Science Development:
An Evaluation Study

DAVID E. DREW

A Technical Report presented to the

NATIONAL BOARD ON GRADUATE EDUCATION

Washington, D.C.

Technical Report Number Four • June 1975

DAVID DREW is a sociologist whose work reflects a continuing interest in higher education, program evaluation, and research methodology. He has extensive experience with multivariate statistical analysis of survey data and the application of computers to the social sciences.

Before becoming Project Director for the NBGE Science Development Study, Mr. Drew had been Associate Director for Information Systems of the American Council on Education Office of Research. Prior to that, he was an Associate in Education at Harvard University, from which he received his Ph.D.

Since completing the study he has joined the Rand Corporation as a Senior Information Scientist.

Library of Congress Cataloging in Publication Data

Drew, David E.
  Science development.

  (Technical report—National Board on Graduate Education; no. 4)
  "A technical report presented to the National Board on Graduate Education."
  Includes bibliographical references.
  1. Science—Study and teaching (Higher)—United States. 2. Research—United States.
3. Universities and colleges—United States. 4. U.S. National Science Foundation. I. Title.
II. Series: National Board on Graduate Education. Technical report—National Board on
Graduate Education; no. 4.
Q183.3.A1D73   507'.1173   75-5929
ISBN 0-309-02329-7

Available from
Printing and Publishing Office
National Academy of Sciences
2101 Constitution Avenue, N.W.
Washington, D.C. 20418

Printed in the United States of America

Highlights

Quantitative analyses of longitudinal data, supplemented by site visits, were used to evaluate the impact of the NSF Science Development program. Setting as its twin goals a dramatic upgrading in the science capabilities of second-tier universities and a broader geographical distribution of scientific talent throughout the nation, this funding program awarded over $230 million to selected universities during the 1960s.

Several technical decisions were made at the outset to help isolate the unique effects of Science Development. First, wherever possible, the data gathered for this study covered the 15 years from 1958 through 1972. Second, all (nonfunded) doctorate-producing universities in the country were used as controls. Third, the three science fields that received the largest share of Science Development funds—physics, chemistry, and mathematics—were analyzed, as was the nonfunded control field of history. Finally, to define "quality science education" in American graduate schools, multiple indicators (i.e., multiple criteria) were used.

The major findings:

1. *Faculty Size*   National Science Foundation funds helped departments in all three science fields to enlarge their faculties. In physics and chemistry, this increase in faculty size was limited to the public sector (Chapter 5).

2. *Faculty Mobility*   An analysis of senior faculty mobility in the field of physics showed that the funded institutions did not develop by recruiting extensively from the leading physics departments.

iii

3. *Scholarly Productivity*   Science Development funding had a positive effect on scholarly productivity as measured by rates of publication in key journals. That is, the funded departments registered an increase in the number of articles published by their faculty members in journals that have the most impact. This increase, however, was largely a function of the growth in faculty size; the effects on the publication rate of the individual faculty members were minimal (Chapter 6).

4. *Graduate Student Enrollment and Quality*   Receipt of a grant was not closely related to increases in graduate student enrollments. Funded departments, however, were able to attract higher quality graduate students (as measured by an improvement in the scores of first-year graduate students on the Graduate Record Examination), though there was no change in the quality of graduate students if one judges by the selectivity of their baccalaureate institutions (Chapter 7).

5. *Ph.D. Production*   Although Science Development funds increased the production of Ph.D.s in physics, in mathematics that effect was felt only in the public sector, not the private. In chemistry, no impact at all was apparent (Chapter 8).

6. *Postdoctorate Employment*   Ph.D.s from funded institutions differed very little from Ph.D.s from nonfunded institutions with respect to the attractiveness of the jobs they took, whether in academe or outside of academe, after receiving the degree. New Ph.D.s in mathematics from private Science Development institutions were somewhat more successful than those from (private) control institutions in getting positions at high-quality universities (Chapter 8).

Foreword

This technical report on the Science Development program, by David Drew, is an experiment in institutional evaluation. Through the program, the National Science Foundation hoped to enable selected universities to improve substantially the quality of their resources for science education and research. The purpose was to develop the competence of the funded institutions in preparing research scholars (as certified by their awarding of the Doctor of Philosophy degree) and in conducting research projects (as evidenced by their receipt of research grants).

The institutions eligible to apply for the Science Development program when it was initiated in 1965 were those considered to be in the "second tier" with respect to quality and reputation in science education. The leading research universities in the country (the so-called "top 20") were excluded from participation, as were institutions deemed to be too weak to advance rapidly. The institutions selected, then, were those that seemed to have potential for developing their science capability markedly in a rather short period of time. Presumably with the assistance of a Science Development grant, these institutions would advance toward excellence; thus, the National Science Foundation hoped to broaden the base of outstanding science competence available to the federal government for its national purposes and to the citizens of the United States. Science Development had as its goal institution building.

The program was by no means unique. Late in the 1940s, both the Carnegie Corporation of New York and The Rockefeller Foundation had made grants designed to help certain universities to expand their programs, to achieve a higher level of quality, and to set standards of excellence that would guide other universities. In the 1950s, the Ford Foundation, with its Challenge Grants, supported a similar endeavor. What was different in 1965 was that this new enterprise in institution building was undertaken by an agency of the federal government.

Dr. Drew was given the problem of how to evaluate the accomplishments of the Science Development program. What impact did the grants have upon the recipient institutions? Did they make possible the achievement of a new level of excellence in science education and research? Did the recipients in fact develop into centers of excellence by reason of these grants? These were the questions to which Dr. Drew sought answers.

It should be observed here that it was the National Science Foundation itself that asked for an evaluation of Science Development. The program having been completed, NSF wanted to know what it had accomplished. How had the nation benefited from the selection of 31 institutions to receive University Science Development grants? The National Science Foundation is to be commended for its spirit of self-inquiry and its initiative in requesting an examination of the consequences of its action.

The difficulty in this circumstance is that evaluating institutional accomplishment is no simple matter. More is involved than determining how the infusion of NSF funds affected the quality of student output or the "value added" to student input, or the quality of particular graduate programs. Essentially, the problem was to determine what happened to a university once the impact of Science Development grants began to be felt. Just how does one determine that changes in quality have occurred at a university and that these changes can be traced or attributed to the availability of additional financial resources? What kinds of objective evidence does one look for?

In this study, Dr. Drew has had to develop techniques of evaluation as well as apply these techniques to the problem at hand. I am sure that he would be the last person to claim that the standards he has used to determine the achievements in a particular university over a particular period of time are ultimate and infallible. Nevertheless, I myself believe that, working within the constraints of the available data, Dr. Drew has notably advanced the state of the art of institutional evaluation.

In the years ahead, we who labor in the field of higher education will be confronted as never before with demands of two kinds. First, we shall be asked to justify the belief that quality in science education and research, quality in all higher education and research, is important to the national welfare. And second, we shall be asked to prove that the amount of financial support available to a university is related to the quality of the achievements of that university. I pass over still another issue: If quality

vi

is so important, and if financial support is the key to quality, then who in society should be expected to pay? But those of us who believe strongly in high standards or achievement in higher education shall be expected to demonstrate the social benefits that derive from excellence and to articulate the means to excellence.

No longer can we accept the interrelation between financial support and academic excellence as an article of faith. We must prove beyond a reasonable doubt that this faith is grounded in reason and fact, not in ancient dogma.

I would like to think that, faced with these concerns in the future, we can look back to this study by Dr. Drew and draw from it encouragement: proof that the interrelation is there if we know how to look for it; evidence of quality in an institution, and of its connection with financial support, can be identified.

Institutional evaluation is here to stay. Now we must strive to make it ever more reliable. This study is a start in the right direction.

JOHN D. MILLETT
Chairman of the Panel
Science Development Evaluation Study

December 1974

Preface

At the outset of this endeavor, it was apparent to me that assessing the Science Development program offered a rare and stimulating opportunity to the evaluation researcher. This National Science Foundation program of the 1960s had been a revolutionary experiment in institutional financing. Millions of dollars were poured into a limited number of carefully selected universities with the goal of dramatically improving their graduate science capabilities. The challenge of evaluating Science Development struck me as particularly exciting in two ways.

First, it offered the chance to conduct research that might have some impact on future federal policy. However much I and my colleagues in the research community would like to believe otherwise, the fact of the matter is that most educational research is ignored by policymakers. This study had the potential to become one of the exceptions. For one thing, the program had dispensed significantly more money than most planned interventions in higher education and had done so in a unique, dramatic way. Also, Science Development had only recently been terminated, and its memory was still fresh; many scientists and policymakers were asking questions about its effectiveness and about the lessons that might be learned from it. Moreover, the study had been requested by the evaluation unit of the National Science Foundation itself—an encouraging sign. The study was housed in the National Board on Graduate Education (NBGE), which in turn is housed in the National Research Council. The sponsorship of the study by these groups,[1] each of which carries weight in

[1]Financially, this research was supported in its entirety by the evaluation unit of the National Science Foundation under Contract C 310, Task Order 263.

ix

the academic and scientific communities, meant that the results would reach a wide and interested audience.

The second challenge was methodological. The field of assessment research is replete with what statisticians refer to as type I and type II errors: on the one hand, subjective case studies that infer dubious "effects"; on the other, sophisticated empirical analyses that consistently fail to detect any effects whatsoever. One frequent source of the latter problem is that the funds given under the particular program being evaluated represent only a small drop in a very large bucket insofar as the recipients are concerned. But Science Development was different. Large sums of money (approximately $6 million per school) were given to only a few universities (31 in all) for a specific purpose. If the program worked, its effects should be discernible. Further, Science Development constituted a natural experiment in that some universities received funds while other, roughly comparable, institutions did not.

In short, this study presented the opportunity to conduct a thorough assessment and perhaps to contribute to the development of evaluation methodology. These objectives (combined with some biases of my own as a methodologist) led to certain technical decisions that are discussed at length in this volume. For instance, longitudinal data were deemed essential for the quantitative analyses. In addition, the decision to use multiple criteria of quality made it possible to study differential effects and thus to avoid reducing the study to one general stamp of approval or rejection. At the same time, the quantitative analyses were supplemented with intensive case studies to explore the way these effects operated in the "real world," thereby obviating the danger of turning the study into a self-contained mathematical exercise (as too many multivariate, quantitative studies are). Finally, recognizing the many valid criticisms of assessment studies where the control group provided an inappropriate comparison, we decided to use all major doctorate-producing universities in the nation as the controls.

Conducting the study did, indeed, turn out to be an exciting and challenging enterprise. As the reader will see, we found that Science Development had a number of effects—some good, some bad. It is our hope that some of the techniques developed here will prove useful to other researchers and that the results of this study will be a guide for future federal policy. With that goal in mind, the National Board on Graduate Education, with the assistance of the study's Advisory Panel, has issued a companion volume to this report in which the policy implications of the research results are spelled out.[2]

---

[2]National Board on Graduate Education, *Science Development, University Development, and the Federal Government* (Washington, D.C., National Academy of Sciences, 1975).

ACKNOWLEDGMENTS

A number of people made valuable contributions to the successful completion of this project.

My primary debt is to my support staff. Each person on the project team was highly qualified, devoted to the research effort, and so competent in carrying out his or her duties that we were able to complete a very large study in a relatively short time.

Margo Jackson filled the central role of Project Assistant, a title vague enough to allow me to delegate to her an extremely varied—and demanding—set of responsibilities that included overseeing all secretarial and clerical work, making the logistical preparations for the Advisory Panel meetings and the site visits, and coordinating the retrieval of graduate student information as described in Chapter 7. In addition, Margo made an important substantive contribution to the research effort by participating in several site visits and by leading one site-visit team.

It was obvious at the outset that we would need a senior computer programmer with an unusual combination of talents: someone with a sophisticated knowledge of multivariate statistical packages who could program efficiently in several computer languages and manipulate exceedingly large data files. After a three-month search, during which we rejected innumerable candidates who had some but not all of these skills, we found Ronald Karpf. Ron's splendid performance was crucial to the success of the project. At one level he participated in the dialogue about appropriate statistical techniques and contributed many valuable ideas. At another, he developed the master file tapes. Most impressive of all was his ability to push an extraordinary amount of material through the Academy's computer in a very short period of time.

Edward Dolbow was initially hired for two months as leader of the library retrieval effort described in Appendix B. After observing his outstanding performance in that job, we persuaded him to stay an additional eight months, to the end of the study. During that period he acted as a key research assistant and troubleshooter. Among the many analyses that reflect his time and effort are the faculty mobility analysis; the school by school review of residual scores; the analysis of the differential effects of funds for personnel, equipment, and facilities; and the analysis of the baccalaureate origins of graduate students.

Marilyn Block brought tremendous skill to her job as research assistant. Her first contribution was to help us review the relative feasibility of library retrieval of journal data and decide on the use to be made of the publication information provided by the Institute for Scientific Information. Later, she was extremely successful in locating secondary sources of data, assessing their relative merits, and retrieving the information needed to construct the study master file. For example, she was instrumental in putting together the data on federal support for science, graduate enrollments, and faculty size.

It was not possible for me as Project Director to lead each site-visit team and at the same time meet my other responsibilities in the project. Dr. Joan Creager, a biologist with considerable experience at interviewing college administrators, took much of that burden from my shoulders by heading the teams to some of the universities. Not only did she very successfully conduct these site visits but in addition her observations—reflecting a delicate balance between idealism and cynicism—were trenchant, perceptive, and wise.

We were fortunate to be able to draw upon the considerable expertise of Laura Kent, who edited this manuscript (and the companion policy report). Her revisions added to whatever clarity this report has.

Two assistants, James Bliffen and Carol Cini, were hired to work with Ed Dolbow on the library retrieval effort. This task, though tedious, was vital to the success of the project; happily, Jim and Carol brought to it the necessary combination of intelligent judgment and conscientious hard work.

At various points in the course of the project, additional secretarial and clerical help was required. Eunice Watson, Jeffrey Shaffer, and Ann Davis contributed significantly to the preparation of the final manuscript.

The Science Development Study Advisory Panel—and in particular its Chairman, Dr. John D. Millett—made numerous contributions to the successful completion of this project:

John D. Millett, Vice President and Director, Management Division, Academy for Educational Development, Inc., *Chairman*
Donald Campbell, Professor of Psychology, Northwestern University
Paul F. Chenea, Vice President, Research Laboratories, General Motors Technical Center, General Motors Corporation
Robert F. Christy, Provost, California Institute of Technology
J. Patrick Crecine, Professor of Political Science, University of Michigan
Hans Laufer, Professor of Biology, University of Connecticut
J. Ross MacDonald, Professor of Physics, University of North Carolina
Lincoln Moses, Dean of Graduate Studies, Stanford University

This study owes a special vote of appreciation to John Millett. Dr. Millett provided effective leadership to the Advisory Panel; he participated in a number of the site visits; he was that chief architect of the companion policy report; he provided guidance and advice on both substantive and procedural matters. In short, he was an invaluable resource for the study staff.

xii

The other panel members contributed in a variety of ways: attending panel meetings, taking part in site visits, and so forth. Donald Campbell, Lincoln Moses, and J. Patrick Crecine—all specialists in methodology—made many valuable suggestions toward the final methodology. In short, the combined inputs of the Advisory Panel members were substantial, helping to shape the research reported in this volume. Finally, the Advisory Panel acted as a task force in drafting the companion volume to this technical report, *Science Development, University Development, and Higher Education*, in which the findings from the study are summarized and the policy implications are elaborated.

This research was supported by the evaluation unit of the National Science Foundation headed by Harry Piccariello. The project monitor was William Commins. These men were helpful and encouraging throughout the study. For example, they assisted us in obtaining whatever data were needed from various departments of the Foundation. Dr. Commins, a statistician, also made many cogent suggestions on both the substance and methodology of the study; it was an unusual pleasure to have a project monitor so knowledgeable about the technical issues we encountered. In addition, Joseph Carabino, an NSF official who was with the Science Development program from its inception, helped us to obtain a variety of data on the administration of the grants. Fred Stafford, recently hired to administer the Science Development program, was also very helpful on a number of occasions.

Several former Science Development officials, no longer with the Foundation, offered advice and suggestions about the nature and significance of this funding experiment. They included Denzel Smith, John Major, and Lou Levin (who acted as a special consultant, reviewing some of our statistical analyses in light of his substantive knowledge of the program). The many other professional colleagues whose advice helped shape this research include Lyle Lanier, Charles Kidd, Robert Hume, Grace Carter and Robert Hoffman. A number of valuable suggestions were contributed by members of the National Board on Graduate Education, who reviewed this study at each of the NBGE meetings held in the past two years.

The contributions of several NBGE and NRC staff members should be acknowledged. David W. Breneman, staff director of the NBGE, acted as a liaison with the Board; he also conducted some of the early negotiations about this evaluation study with the National Science Foundation. Herb Soldz, head of the Commission on Human Resources Data Processing Unit, contributed his help on a variety of occasions. Our analytic effort benefited greatly from the data-handling system developed by his unit. This system includes a set of well-designed and well-documented data tapes and an extremely effective compiler created to maximize efficiency in the use of those tapes. Clarebeth Cunningham was an effective guide through the maze of information in the NRC Doctorate Record File.

Finally, I would like to dedicate this effort to my wife, Ann.

December 1974   David E. Drew

CONTENTS

Science Development:

An Evaluation Study

1 Introduction

This report presents the findings of an extensive evaluation study of the National Science Foundation's Science Development program. The federal government launched this massive funding program in 1965. Intended to improve graduate science education in the United States, it was based on three innovative concepts. First a group of *second-tier* universities—those that ranked just below the "top 20" in science quality—should be given substantial infusions of funds to propel them into becoming "centers of excellence."

Second, support should be given to the *institution* to be targeted at science areas. This pattern contrasts with previous patterns of federal funding directed at individual researchers or projects. Such awards, it was argued, tended to create scientific prima donnas with little institutional loyalty and benefited the institution only indirectly, if at all.

The final concept was that *every region* in the country should be served by an outstanding university, a notion strongly supported by Presidents Kennedy and Johnson. Previous national studies, notably the Seaborg report (1960),[1] had commented on the intense concentration of federal support for science in a few select universities, disproportionately clustered in the Northeast.

Although the structure of the funding program changed several times, the major subprogram was University Science Development (USD), under

[1]President's Science Advisory Committee, *Scientific Progress, the Universities, and the Federal Government* (Washington, D.C.: The White House, November 1960).

1

which 31 universities received over $177 million. These institutions had to give evidence of having an overall development scheme that included extensive plans for the sciences. Technically, matching funds were not required, but the institution was expected to make a significant financial contribution as part of the program. The National Science Foundation (NSF) excluded from consideration not only existing centers of excellence but also institutions that it felt lacked sufficient strength to develop rapidly into such centers.

There were two other subprograms relating to graduate science education under which limited grants were given for less ambitious development plans: Department Science Development (DSD) and Special Science Development (SSD). Both are described in greater detail in Chapter 2.

As noted above, the Science Development program differed from most federal support of university activities in that the money did not go directly to individual scientists or scholars and their projects, but to institutions. The program also differed from other more traditional forms of institutional support such as formula grants—notably, in the relatively large size of the awards. Science Development funds were used for hiring new faculty, graduate student support, the development of interdisciplinary institutes, the construction of major new facilities, and so forth.

Federal expenditures for science research have been commonplace since World War II and the spectacular technical success of the Manhattan project. Shortly after the war, the case for continued government support of basic science research was made by Vannevar Bush[2] and others; the major science organization to grow out of this federal concern was the National Science Foundation. Subsequently, in the late 1950s (with the voyage of *Sputnik*), science education became a national priority. That period spawned a wide array of measures in support of science education (e.g., the National Defense Education Act).

With the passage of time, the government grew increasingly reluctant simply to underwrite projects with a blank check and, concomitantly, became more concerned with monitoring federally supported programs. Thus, for example, the landmark 1965 Elementary and Secondary Education Act contained measures requiring that the projects it was launching be evaluated.

Often, "evaluation" means no more than a cursory field trip followed by armchair speculation resulting in a plea for more funds, thinly disguised as an accountability report. Against this background, the request by the NSF evaluation unit for a major empirical assessment of the effects of Science Development stands in sharp relief.

[2]Vannevar Bush, *Science, The Endless Frontier: A Report to the President* (Washington, D.C.: U.S. Government Printing Office, July 1945).

2

In 1971 (the same year that saw the demise of the Science Development program), NSF asked the National Academy of Sciences to conduct this evaluative study under funding from the Foundation. The most appropriate location for the study within the complex Academy structure was felt to be the National Board on Graduate Education. The Board, chaired by David Henry, was established by the Conference Board on Associated Research Councils to "provide a means for an unbiased, thorough analysis of graduate education today."[3] Both Academy officials and National Board members agreed that it was vital to underscore at the outset the necessity for an objective, scientific assessment. Further, both groups agreed that the study would be relevant to their charters as long as the focus was not on a limited evaluation or audit of the funding program but rather on a more general study that would have wider policy implications.

The basic goal, of course, was to examine the effectiveness of this form of institutional support: Did the funded institutions develop their science capabilities at a significantly greater rate in the past decade than did nonfunded institutions (including the "top 20")? What were the effects of the program's emphasis on geographical dispersion? What was the impact, if any, on nonfunded departments in institutions that received a grant? What happened in the funded universities when these massive government grants ended? What were the differential effects of funds given under the USD and DSD subprograms?

To answer these questions, we had to tackle the thorny issue of defining "quality" science education. What does this term mean as applied to graduate schools in the United States? It rapidly became clear that no single index would do; we needed to use multiple indicators of quality; i.e., multiple criteria. It is hoped that this research will contribute toward a definition of "quality graduate education" in terms that can be operationalized for empirical research.

Several principles guided the development of the methodology for this evaluation study:

1. The research combined two approaches: (a) multivariate analyses of quantitative data on institutions and (b) selected case studies, carried out by site visits.

2. All too frequently, evaluation studies of complex projects try to reduce their conclusions to one general stamp of approval or rejection. The goal of this study was both more complex and more difficult: to trace the differential effects of funding patterns upon a number of outcomes represented by various indices of science excellence. The ultimate goal

[3]*Graduate Education: Purposes, and Potential: A Report of the National Board on Graduate Education* (Washington, D.C.: NBGE, November 1972), p. v.

was to develop policy recommendations that might guide future funding of graduate science education.

3. Discerning the unique effects of Science Development required both longitudinal data and complex statistical techniques. Therefore, wherever possible, the information gathered for this study was based on the 15 years from 1958 through 1972. Thus, not only did we span the entire lifetime of Science Development (1965–1971) but also we collected data on trends under way before 1965.

4. To allow for thorough and meaningful comparison of trends in the funded institutions with trends in other universities, we collected and analyzed data not just on funded institutions and a few select controls but on every major doctorate-producing institution in the nation. Thus, the sample consisted of all universities rated by Roose and Andersen in their 1970 evaluation of graduate education in the United States.[4] This procedure enabled us to compare the Science Development institutions with control institutions of roughly similar initial quality, as well as with those institutions excluded from the grant program either because they were already considered excellent or because their science capabilities fell well below those of the funded institutions.

At this juncture it might be helpful to indicate how this technical report is organized. Chapter 2 contains a detailed history and description of the NSF Science Development program. Chapter 3 spells out the methods used in both the quantitative analyses and the site visits and indicates the reasons underlying several major technical decisions (e.g., sampling techniques and the heavy reliance on longitudinal data).

The site visits provided a rich resource for understanding many of the relationships uncovered in the quantitative analyses. In addition, some general observations about the impact of the program and about indicators of success and nonsuccess were made during those visits. Those observations are presented in Chapter 4.

The next four chapters report the results of the quantitative analyses. A separate chapter is devoted to each of the parameters of science excellence. Chapter 5 describes the changes in faculty size resulting from the program; a special section examines the validity of the charge leveled by some critics that Science Development funds did no more than permit recipient institutions to develop by stealing top talent from the leading institutions. In Chapter 6 the research productivity of Science Development faculty is explored through an analysis of publication rates in leading journals. (The procedure used to select the leading journals in each field is described in Appendix B.) Chapter 7 explores the effects of Science

[4]Kenneth D. Roose and Charles J. Andersen, *A Rating of Graduate Programs* (Washington, D.C.: American Council on Education, 1970).

4

Development funding on the graduate student population in terms of enrollments, test scores, and baccalaureate origins. The program's impact on Ph.D. production is discussed in Chapter 8; because the *over*production of Ph.D.s—and their subsequent underemployment—has become a hot topic in the last several years and because the Science Development program was accused by some of contributing to the oversupply of Ph.D.s, a special analysis of the nature of postdoctorate employment was carried out and is discussed here. The final chapter summarizes the methods and major findings of the study.

There are three appendices. Appendix A lists the schools comprising each sample group for the study. In Appendix B the methods used to select the journals for the productivity analysis (Chapter 6) are presented. Finally, Appendix C reports the findings from a series of special supplementary analyses of the data.

This technical report is the first of two documents to emerge from the study. The second is a National Board on Graduate Education policy statement written by a task force comprising the members of the study's Advisory Panel, headed by John Millett. That statement summarizes the findings from the study, discusses some of its implications for graduate education in the United States, and enumerates policy guidelines that should prove valuable for future funding programs.

2 The NSF Science Development Program

Just as Research Applied to National Needs (RANN) has been the dominant new NSF program of the 1970s, so Science Development was the dominant new NSF program of the 1960s. In basic philosophy it represented a radical departure from previous federal funding for science. As indicated in Chapter 1, the program embodied three innovative concepts:

1. Funding via institutional rather than project support;
2. Funding of "second-tier" institutions (i.e., those not yet considered excellent) together with deliberate exclusion of those universities in the "top 20";
3. Strong emphasis on geographical dispersion of the funded institutions.

To give a complete frame of reference in which to present the results of this evaluation study, the history and development of this NSF program will be traced.

Perhaps the major impetus for a program of this type was *Scientific Progress, the Universities, and the Federal Government*, a statement by the President's Science Advisory Committee that appeared in November 1960. A major conclusion of this report, known as the Seaborg report (after Glenn T. Seaborg, then Chancellor of the University of California, Berkeley, and chairman of the committee), follows:

6

Equally with the importance of sustaining what is already outstanding, we urge the importance for the country of an increase in the number of universities in which first-rate research and graduate teaching go forward together. The growth of science requires more places with superior faculties and outstanding groups of students. Existing strong institutions cannot fully meet the nation's future needs. It is true that experience is casting doubt on some conservative notions about the optimum size of the university, and the universities which are already great are larger than they expected to be ten years ago. But there is a limit to such growth, and we must hope that where there were only a handful of generally first-rate academic centers of science a generation ago and may be as many as fifteen or twenty today, there will be thirty or forty in another fifteen years. Timely and determined support to the rising centers will be repaid many times over in service to society.[1]

This observation was formalized in the Third of the general recommendations:

It is of equal importance to increase support for rising centers of science. Over the next fifteen years the United States should seek to double the number of universities doing generally excellent work in basic research and graduate education.[2]

This notion, first articulated while Eisenhower was still president, was subsequently endorsed and expanded by both the Kennedy and the Johnson administrations. The program took more definite form during Johnson's administration and was consistent with his philosophy of geographic diffusion of funds. In fact a 1965 Executive Order on that subject was closely tied to the disbursement of NSF funds for University Science Development.

The Science Development program was formally announced in March 1964; the first grants under the program were awarded during fiscal year 1965. These awards, to eight universities (two of which, Case and Western Reserve, subsequently merged) were major institutional grants designed to upgrade a number of science departments in each of the recipient institutions. At that point, NSF was awarding funds only in the mode that subsequently came to be known as the University Science Development subprogram. In an excellent article reviewing the history of Science Development, Howard E. Page, a former administrator of the program, discusses the philosophy underlying institutional support:

Heretofore, NSF programs had been concerned mainly with the development of individual scientists, the expansion of scientific knowledge, and the building of research laboratories. Valuable as these programs were, their aim was to strengthen science per se; they did not necessarily aim at strengthening the institutions that furnish the home for science. To think institutionally meant to think more broadly than the foundation had done before. An institutional program must provide a means of integrating the various components of the customary kinds of support into an organic unit. Activities in natural science and engineering

[1] President's Science Advisory Committee, *Scientific Progress, the Universities, and the Federal Government* (Washington, D.C.: The White House, November 1960), pp. 14–15.
[2] *Ibid.*, p. 28.

must be viewed in relation to those in the humanities and social sciences; the ways by which an institution's educational and research policies are determined and administered must be understood; the present and potential sources of the institution's financial support must be known; and the hopes and plans of the institution's its special culture, and its relation to its social and intellectual environment must be perceived. In other words, a foundation official must put himself behind the desk of the college or university president, at the same time remembering that, as a guardian of federal tax funds, he is concerned about the general health of science rather than the advancement of one institution alone.[3]

While Science Development was a significant innovation, its developers drew to a certain degree on the experience of the Ford Foundation in its Challenge Grant program. There were, however, differences between the two programs. First, the Ford grants were restricted to private institutions and were given only to schools the foundation invited. Second, Ford grants were given to both universities and four-year colleges in larger amounts than were provided by the NSF program; for example, the amount awarded to some universities went as high as $25 million, roughly three times as much as the largest Science Development grant. Finally, the Ford money was not restricted to science fields.

A federal precedent for institutional support of higher education is provided by the 1887 Hatch Act, administered by the Department of Agriculture. This Act established the experimental stations at land-grant colleges to advance the agricultural sciences and to disseminate information, particularly among rural communities, about discoveries in the field.

STRUCTURE OF SCIENCE DEVELOPMENT

In the first years of the program, it became apparent that the pattern followed in awarding the early grants would not fit every institutional situation encountered by NSF. As a result, the program underwent several reorganizations that resulted in a series of subprograms.

The primary form of institutional funding—awards of three-year grants amounting to approximately $4 million each (with two-year supplementary increments)—became known as the University Science Development (USD) subprogram. The USD approach essentially embodied the Science Development philosophy; under this subprogram, by far the greatest amount of money was awarded ($177 million to 31 institutions).

A second subprogram, the Special Science Development (SSD) subprogram, first awarded grants in fiscal year 1966. The purpose of these special grants was to fund institutions that originally had applied for a USD grant but

[3] Howard E. Page, "The Science Development Program," in *Science Policy and the University,* ed. Harold Orlans (Washington, D.C.: Brookings Institution, 1968), p. 103.

that the Foundation judged lacking in sufficient overall science strength to justify a total institutional award. Thus, SSD grants were given to one or two science departments instead of the five or six that the institution might originally have proposed in their USD application. Under this subprogram, a total of 11 grants were awarded in the total amount of $11,937,000.

The third program, the Departmental Science Development (DSD) subprogram was announced in October 1966 and became operational in January 1967. Ultimately, 73 grants averaging about $600,000 each (for a total of $41,932,210) were given to departments in 62 institutions. This subprogram served several successive purposes. At first, it was intended in part to boost institutions in urban areas that otherwise lacked good science facilities. Although eventually the Foundation funded schools in all types of demographic settings, a sizable number of the DSD grants did go to institutions in urban centers of 250,000 or more. Perhaps the key characteristic of this subprogram was the funding of a single department, occasionally two, that showed the capacity to develop excellence in an institution that otherwise demonstrated mediocre science capabilities. Departmental Science Development awards began as proposals for support of a single department, unlike the SSD grants that resulted from USD proposals that were scaled down by NSF.

It was further provided, in fiscal year 1969, that universities that had demonstrated sufficient success under the first DSD award could apply for a second, and sometimes a third, DSD grant for new departments.

According to William V. Consolazio,[4] in his report on the subprogram for fiscal year 1969; "This change was designed primarily to encourage each institution with the potential for significant growth and development to progress at a rate commensurate with its own needs and resources."

In its early days, the DSD subprogram was also seen as a way of significantly increasing the number of awards made to the social sciences. Consolazio comments on this issue: "With respect to strengthening . . . science, it becomes increasingly clear that the social sciences are candidates for some special national effort and that the development technique seems to be tailor-made for this purpose."[5] He goes on to argue for the creation of a new special program for the development of the social sciences, but such a program was never brought into existence under Science Development.

A final innovative characteristic of the DSD subprogram was the manner in which DSD funds were used to encourage the development of interdisciplinary institutes, programs, and so forth.

[4] William V. Consolazio, "Departmental Science Development," in *Annual Report: Institutional Support Programs for the Fiscal Year 1969* (Washington, D.C.: National Science Foundation, 1970), p. 42.
[5] *Ibid.*, p. 50.

9

Yet another subprogram, the College Science Improvement Program (COSIP), was created under Science Development in 1967. Because COSIP was aimed at undergraduate education only, it is not part of this evaluation, which has focused exclusively on federal support for graduate education. College Science Improvement Program, in fact, was the subject of a previous evaluation study conducted at the American Council on Education.[6]

These four programs—USD, DSD, SSD, and COSIP—constituted the Science Development institutional funding program. During the same period, NSF administered two different, but related, institutional support programs: Institutional Grants for Science and the Graduate Science Facilities Program. Under the former, relatively small formula grants were given to a large number of universities; the amount awarded to each institution was calculated as a function of the other federal support for science it received. Institutional Grants for Science differed from Science Development in several ways: the small size of each award, the large number of awards given, and the use of a formula to determine amounts of awards, with no other attempt at systematic evaluation of an institution's science strength. As its name implies, the Graduate Science Facilities Program was limited to providing funds—matching grants, in particular—to aid in constructing new science buildings.

SELECTION OF RECIPIENTS

Typically, informal discussions between the Foundation and each potential applicant institution preceded the development of a formal proposal by the institution. Page reports that well over 200 informal inquiries were received shortly after the announcement of the program.[7] Once the institution submitted a formal proposal, the Foundation began a lengthy evaluation, which relied in great part on peer review—that is, review by scientists and scholars outside the Foundation—as well as on internal review. The first step was soliciting the opinions of outside experts about the proposal itself. Once this hurdle had been cleared, the Foundation sent a site-visit team to spend several days at the institution. Typically, this team comprised not only Foundation officials but also several outstanding scientists in the fields being proposed for funding and one or more experienced university administrators. After the site visit, each member submitted a lengthy report evaluating the proposal, the science capabilities of the university, and the

[6] David E. Drew, *On the Allocation of Federal Funds for Science Education,* ACE Research Reports, Vol. 5, No. 7 (Washington, D.C.: American Council on Education, 1970); *A Study of the NSF College Science Improvement Program,* ACE Research Reports, Vol. 6, No. 4 (Washington, D.C.: American Council on Education, 1971).
[7] Page, *op. cit.* p. 106.

overall administrative strength of the school. Further internal NSF administrative review was followed by a recommendation to a special panel of
experts that advised the Foundation on Science Development. If this group
recommended that a USD proposal be approved, the school typically
received about $4 million over a three-year period.

At the completion of the initial award, each USD recipient was
encouraged to apply for supplementary funding to cover an additional two
years. They were expected to submit a full formal proposal documenting
their plans for those two years and including a statement of progress under
the initial years of USD support. The evaluation procedures for the
supplementary proposal closely paralleled those applied to the original
proposal. Of the 31 USD recipients, 30 received a supplementary extension
of funds. Thus, the typical USD recipient was awarded $6 million over a
five-year period.

In both proposals, the institution was expected to indicate (1) a clearly
defined development scheme for the sciences that was part of a larger
institutional plan, (2) the sources of university support that would
complement the funds being provided by the Foundation, and (3) plans for
the continuation of the momentum provided by the proposed funding.

Since SSD grants resulted from USD proposals, the procedures followed
in evaluating those applications were identical except that supplementary
funds were not extended to those institutions.

Departmental Science Development proposals were evaluated in much
the same way as proposals for the larger grants, but in a scaled-down
manner. In the annual report for fiscal year 1967, the DSD evaluation
procedures are described as "quite comprehensive," involving "a great
deal of time and effort on the part of many people":

Serious consideration is given to each proposal in order to assure that sound judgment is
behind each recommended action. Many factors are involved in evaluating proposals, such as:
soundness and feasibility of the proposed development plan; commitment of the institution
and its leadership to the plan; quality of the department leadership and its dedication to the
plan; nature and quality of present faculty, students, and the department's research programs;
adequacy of [the] department's facilities and equipment; quality of related departments,
particularly those associated with or impinging on the plan; intellectual, financial, and regional
capability for attraction of high-quality new faculty and students; and, appropriateness and
adequacy of the proposed budget and of the institution's financial participation in the plan plus
its capability to sustain the development program.[8]

A key factor in assessing Science Development is the set of criteria used
to evaluate the original proposals; presumably these criteria bear some
resemblance to those used in this evaluation study. Howard Page comments on this issue, citing a critic of the program, Saunders MacLane, who
labeled it "vague, because it has no objective criteria." According to

[8] *Annual Report: Institutional Support Programs for the Fiscal Year 1967* (Washington, D.C.:
National Science Foundation 1968), p. 7.

MacLane, "a center of excellence usually requires some tradition and certainly requires a sufficient concentration (a 'critical mass') of first-rate scientists."[9] Page goes on to say that "the Foundation knows that 'objective criteria' are inadequate for measuring excellence, a fact especially bothersome to scientists; nevertheless, they have managed to get over that hurdle and begun to think like humanists."[10]

In short, the process that the Foundation used to evaluate proposals was aimed at excluding those universities felt to lack a sufficient basis for developing excellence under funding. At the outset, those schools already regarded as exhibiting excellence were excluded, although all concerned were careful never to release a public list of this "top 20" group. (There is some indication that such a list was circulated internally at NSF). Perhaps a statement attributed to Alvin Weinberg best summarizes the distinction between the "top 20" and the "second-tier" institutions: "An excellent school is one I will send my son to, and a good school is one I will send my nephew to."

Certainly, the decisions that faced the Foundation in evaluating proposals bear a great resemblance to the decisions faced by researchers in evaluating the program. In that vein, a comment reported at the conclusion of Page's article is particularly opposite:

The evaluation of the effects of development grants was recognized as important but difficult. (One official declared forcefully that the government and the research community were more interested in spending money than in carefully evaluating what had been accomplished by money already spent. "Now, the government is spending $15 billion a year in RDT&E (Research, Development, Training, and Evaluation) . . . [and] how much of that is going into an analysis of how our RDT&E is done? Peanuts." "If they knew what they were achieving," it was suggested sarcastically, "they might spend less and that is an argument for not knowing.") Some marks of failure—such as a university president's moving on to another job after securing the grant or putting all of his free money into buildings rather than people— were more evident than signs of success. Progress was not, by itself, proof that it had been caused by the grant, as many school receiving grants were on the upswing and would have improved in any event. Furthermore, a good plan, prepared not just by the president's office (as was too common with the poorer plans) but by the genuine involvement of a broad group of faculty, might be as responsible for an institution's progress as the grant itself.[11]

SCIENCE DEVELOPMENT AWARDS

For a full understanding of the analyses reported in subsequent chapters, the reader should be aware of which institutions received Science

[9] Saunders MacLane, "Leadership and Quality in Science," in *Basic Research and National Goals,* A Report to the House Committee on Science and Astronautics by the National Academy of Sciences, 89th Congr. 1st sess (March 1965), p. 200.
[10] Page, *op. cit.* p. 109.
[11] *Ibid.,* pp. 118–19.

Development grants, what kind of grant they received, and the amount of money involved.[12] Table 2-1, 2-2, and 2-3 present financial information for all recipients of USD, DSD, or SSD grants. For each recipient institution, the following information is given: the date of the initial award, total initial funds, the date of the supplementary award, total supplementary funds. For the DSD and SSD grants, the funded fields are listed.

The dimensions of the funding program can be quickly grasped by inspecting these tables. Some additional summary data: in the USD sub-program the most heavily funded fields were physics ($50.3 million), chemistry ($31.5 million), and mathematics ($11.2 million). Also, the breakdown of funds for personnel ($71.6 million), equipment ($65.5 million), and facilities ($39.9 million) is interesting.

Financial data such as those in Table 2-1 give a complete, but rather dry, account of Science Development. A much richer and more interesting picture emerges when one reads the NSF files or visits the recipient institutions, as was done in this study. The funds have produced a number of exciting innovations. For example:

Science Development permitted the University of Virginia to create a Center for Advanced Study in the Sciences through which they were able to hire both distinguished and promising younger scholars. The concept was so successful that they subsequently added other, nonscience fields (using other funds) and changed the name to the Center for Advanced Study.

At Rice University scientists from many departments who had been working separately on problems requiring a systems approach were brought together in a new systems program under Science Development. The program drew upon economists, psychologists, electrical engineers, mathematicians, and so forth.

At the University of Arizona, Science Development funds were used to bolster several physical science departments, notably astronomy. A major portion of the award to Arizona was used for the construction of a 90-in. reflector telescope on neighboring Kitt Peak.

DSD funds were the catalytic factor in the development of an interdisciplinary, research-oriented Ecology Center at Utah State University.

At the University of California, Santa Cruz, DSD funds made possible the development of a theoretical astrophysics thrust in the Astronomy

---

[12] Since the National Science Foundation considers the identities of institutions whose proposals were declined as confidential, no information on the declinations is given in this report.

TABLE 2-1   University Science Development Recipients (funds in thousands of dollars)

Institution	Initial Award		Supplementary Award	
	Date	Amount	Date	Amount
Arizona	07-02-65	$4,045	06-10-69	$3,182
Carnegie-Mellon	05-10-67	4,399	05-26-72	450
Case Western Reserve	—	—	05-31-68	2,160
Case Institute	05-13-65	3,500	—	—
Western Reserve	05-13-65	3,500	—	—
Colorado	06-30-65	3,755	03-31-70	1,676
Duke	12-20-66	2,527	05-26-72	650
Florida	07-02-65	4,240	02-07-69	1,688
Florida State	03-21-68	4,820	05-26-72	1,200
Georgia	08-29-67	3,719	03-31-70	2,276
Indiana	12-20-66	7,886	05-26-72	1,470
Iowa (Iowa City)	08-29-67	5,101	05-20-71	612
Louisiana State	05-31-68	3,787	03-31-70	2,429
Maryland	05-10-67	3,703	05-20-71	652
Michigan State	05-31-68	4,307	05-26-72	1,180
New York University	06-10-69	4,560	05-26-72	1,600
North Carolina	05-10-67	4,995	05-20-71	1,071
North Carolina State	05-19-66	3,555	05-20-71	678
Notre Dame	05-10-67	4,766	05-20-71	451
Oregon	03-05-70	4,000	12-31-69	2,748
Pittsburgh	06-10-69	3,650	05-26-72	800
Polytechnic Institute, Brooklyn	11-03-65	3,332	02-06-69	1,210
Purdue	05-19-66	3,600	05-26-72	300
Rice	06-30-65	2,390	—	—
Rochester	06-30-65	4,500	12-31-69	1,205
Rutgers	05-19-66	3,708	05-20-71	334
Texas	05-20-71	5,000	05-20-71	959
Tulane	05-20-71	3,685	05-20-71	673
USC	11-03-65	4,473	02-07-69	3,000
Vanderbilt	05-10-67	4,053	05-26-72	1,350
Virginia	06-30-65	3,780	06-10-69	1,904
Washington (Seattle)	05-31-68	5,000	05-20-71	906
Washington (St. Louis)	05-13-65	3,919	02-07-69	3,090

Department to complement the existing, applied orientation (based on the nearby location of the Lick Observatory).

The Sociology Department of Washington State University used Science Development funds to develop rapid turn-around survey mechanisms and to create an urban field station for research.

TABLE 2-2   Special Science Development Recipients (funds in thousands of dollars)

Institution	Date	Amount Awarded	Area
Brandeis	03-19-70	$1,900	chemistry, physics
Connecticut	03-31-70	145	environmental science
Kansas State	06-10-69	819	biology
Kentucky	03-20-68	974	mathematics
Nebraska	03-26-69	830	chemistry
New Mexico State	04-12-66	700	mathematics
Northwestern	05-19-70	1,500	urban systems engineering
SUNY Stony Brook	03-19-70	2,000	astronomy and astrophysics
Tennessee	03-20-68	1,450	chemical and metal engineering, physics
Wayne State	05-01-67	919	chemistry
West Virginia University	03-08-67	700	engineering

TABLE 2-3   Departmental Science Development Recipients (funds in dollars)

Institution	Date	Amount Awarded	Area
Alaska	04-30-70	$ 720,000	geology
Arizona State	03-26-69	650,000	solid state science
Boston University	03-05-70	650,000	biological science
Bowling Green	03-26-69	531,900	psychology
Bryn Mawr	05-23-69	403,000	biochemistry
California, San Diego	09-15-70	571,000	economics
California, Santa Barbara	09-15-70	480,000	electrical engineering
California, Santa Cruz	03-26-69	600,000	astronomy
Claremont	05-31-68	491,500	mathematics
	04-09-71	466,000	psychology
Clark	06-12-67	545,070	psychology
	03-26-69	563,740	geography
Clarkson	03-26-69	800,000	chemical engineering
Clemson	03-05-70	650,000	engineering
Colorado School of Mines	04-30-70	700,000	geosci–mineral resources
Colorado State	03-05-70	600,000	civil engineering
CUNY, City College	05-31-68	765,000	physics
CUNY, Hunter College	05-31-68	617,800	biology
Delaware	02-16-68	556,000	physics
Denver	05-31-68	500,000	mathematics
Drexel Institute	06-12-67	527,700	chemical engineering
Emory	09-15-70	562,000	chemistry
Georgetown	04-30-70	460,000	language and linguistics
Hawaii	04-30-70	606,000	chemistry
Houston	09-28-67	420,000	chemical engineering
Illinois, Chicago Circle	05-31-68	545,000	chemistry
Illinois Institute of Technology	03-26-69	800,000	biology
Kent State	03-05-70	400,000	psychology

TABLE 2-3   Continued

Institution	Date	Amount Awarded	Area
Lehigh	09-28-67	550,000	metallurgy and material sciences
	09-17-69	670,000	mechanical engineering and mechanics
Louisiana State, New Orleans	05-31-68	477,800	chemistry
Louisville	05-31-68	500,000	psychology
Marquette	09-28-67	540,000	biology
Massachusetts	04-09-71	582,000	psychology
Michigan Tech.	03-26-69	384,500	engineering
Mississippi	12-29-69	400,000	electrical engineering
Missouri	09-28-67	550,000	physics
Montana	04-09-71	500,000	geology
Nebraska	03-26-69	715,000	physics
New Hampshire	03-05-70	480,000	psychology
New Mexico	06-12-67	550,000	mathematics
Oakland	05-31-68	570,000	engineering
Ohio	02-16-68	563,000	physics
Oklahoma State	03-26-69	665,200	systems science
Oregon State	03-05-70	600,000	chemistry
Rochester	04-09-71	848,000	fundamental studies (multidisciplinary)
RPI	02-16-68	569,000	mathematics
	06-30-69	490,000	chemistry
SMU	02-16-68	600,000	electrical engineering
	03-05-70	550,000	economics
	04-09-71	600,000	anthropology
South Carolina	05-23-69	500,000	chemistry
Stevens Institute	09-17-69	670,000	physics
SUNY, Albany	03-26-69	480,000	mathematics
	09-15-70	525,000	biological sciences
SUNY, Binghamton	05-31-68	500,000	geology
	03-05-70	390,000	economics
Tennessee Tech.	06-12-67	300,000	mechanical engineering
Texas A&M	03-26-69	560,000	chemistry
	09-15-70	458,000	economics
Texas Tech	09-15-70	476,000	electrical engineering
Utah	06-09-69	720,000	physics
	09-15-70	695,000	chemistry
Utah State	05-31-68	550,000	ecology
VPI	09-17-69	500,000	geological sciences
Washington State	05-31-68	550,000	chemical physics
	09-15-70	530,000	sociology
Wesleyan	05-31-68	560,000	physics
William and Mary	03-05-70	610,000	physics
Wisconsin, Milwaukee	02-16-68	550,000	surface studies
Wyoming	02-16-68	477,000	geology
Yale	05-27-71	1,500,000	social sciences
Yeshiva	12-22-69	900,000	physics

Science Development funds to each of the three Triangle Universities in North Carolina help create a regional combined center of excellence. The funds enabled the University of North Carolina at Chapel Hill to become a leader in the quantitative social sciences.

DENOUEMENT OF THE PROGRAM

The impact and the image of Science Development is reflected in the following statement from a recent article about the National Science Foundation.

Institutional support and fellowship grants . . . elevated . . . graduate schools and departments to top rank. Privately, NSF was given much of the credit for the development of the highly regarded astronomy department at the University of Arizona, the mathematics department of Louisiana State University, and the physics departments at Rutgers and the University of Oregon, among others. Arizona alone received $7.2 million from NSF over the past five years.[13]

Talking about the Nixon administration's cutback of funds for higher education, the same article goes on to quote Thomas Jones, President of the University of South Carolina:

When reduction begins, [Jones] said, "A ripple, then a wave, goes down through the pecking order of institutions as they scramble to find new sources of support. The lesser institutions experience an acceleration and disappearance of funds . . . and return to the second-hand, spectator-type science that characterized those institutions prior to World War II.

"One might conclude that these less than superb institutions are not really important to science in our nation," Jones said. "But let me say that nothing could be further from the truth. The future economic health of our nation depends on at least one institution that is excellent in science in every state in our union."[14]

The Science Development program was terminated by the Nixon administration in 1971. The last initial USD awards were made in June 1969; the last supplementary awards were made in 1971, as were the last DSD awards. The final nine USD supplementary awards represented previously impounded funds that were released by the Office of Management and Budget only after considerable lobbying by the institutions involved. Even at that, a total of only $9 million was awarded to those schools although, consistent with earlier supplementary grants, the initial Foundation recommendations had been considerably higher.

[13] Rudy Abramson, "Patron on the Potomac: The National Science Foundation," *Change,* May–June 1971, p. 38.
[14] *Ibid.*, p. 42.

TABLE 2-4 Total Federal Funds for Science to Science Development and Control Institutions, 1963–1972 (in thousands of dollars)

	No.	1963	1964	1965	1966	1967	1968	1969	1970	1971	1972
All Institutions											
Recipients	29	9,981	11,909	14,393	16,902	17,585	17,441	17,543	15,825	17,208	18,401
Controls	17	9,753	10,677	12,383	14,699	14,960	14,724	14,511	13,484	14,845	16,396
Public Institutions											
Recipients	17	9,836	11,642	14,571	17,218	17,216	18,088	16,974	16,183	17,925	18,737
Controls	9	8,715	9,409	11,465	13,657	14,662	14,655	13,936	12,873	14,554	16,082
Private Institutions											
Recipients	12	10,186	12,287	14,142	16,453	18,107	16,525	18,349	15,318	16,192	17,924
Controls	8	10,920	12,104	13,415	15,872	15,295	14,802	15,159	14,171	15,172	16,749

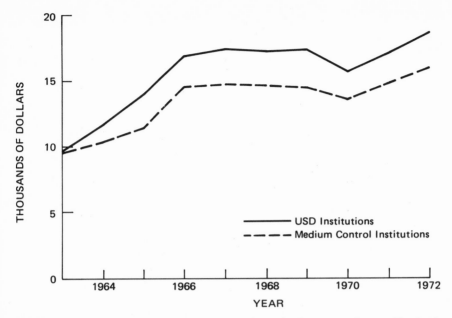

FIGURE 2-1 Total federal funds for science to science development and control institutions, 1963–1972

SCIENCE DEVELOPMENT IN FINANCIAL PERSPECTIVE

As a glance at Table 2-1 to 2-3 indicates, the amounts awarded under Science Development were quite large by most standards; this report is devoted to examining the effects of the grants. It is reasonable to ask at the outset how these magnitudes compared with the total funds being awarded by the federal government for science to these and other institutions. Data on federal support for science per institution are compiled and published annually by the National Science Foundation through its *Committee on Academic Science and Engineering.* Table 2-4 shows the total federal science support per university for each year from 1963 to 1972 for each of two groups: the 31 USD recipients and a control group of comparable institutions.[15] These same data are plotted graphically in Figure 2-1.

An examination of this figure reveals a rather important point. While Science Development funds were large (i.e., millions of dollars), they represented only a small portion of the total federal aid for science that was directed at the recipient institutions during those years. As a result, there are many difficulties involved in assessing the impact of Science Develop-

[15] For a detailed discussion of how the control group was selected, see Chapter 3. Appendix A lists all institutions in both the recipient and control groups (referred to there as "medium controls").

ment funds. That is, in its peak years, the program was providing about $1 or $2 million annually to each recipient institution, out of total federal awards to that school in the neighborhood of $15 million. Thus, even if these funds had significant effects, detecting them is quite a challenge in light of the huge amount of other forms of federal support. Conversely, any effects that are found will serve to indicate that the mechanism for directing and awarding these Science Development funds was particularly effective.[16]

[16] In addition to these problems, a related methodological challenge to an effective evaluation should be noted. An ever-increasing body of literature reporting research about the effects of various forms of intervention (e.g., schooling) is coming to the conclusion that change strategies have no effect. In a sense, this is the general conclusion of such major studies as the Coleman report [James S. Coleman *et al.*, *Equality of Educational Opportunity* (Washington, D.C.: U.S. Government Printing Office, 1966)], Christopher Jencks *et al.*, *Inequality: A Reassessment of the Effect of Family and Schooling in America* (New York: Basic Books, 1972), and the work of Alexander W. Astin (see especially Astin, "Undergraduate Achievement and Institutional 'Excellence,'" *Science*, 16 August 1968, pp. 661–668). Essentially, all of these researchers used multivariate techniques to examine the effects of the educational environment while controlling for input: They found that when input was statistically controlled, the unique effects of environment on output were minimal, if visible. A case can be made, however, that these conclusions are based on faulty methods: the lack of longitudinal data in one case, a blurring of input and environment in another, and so forth. That is, while we shall be using multivariate techniques, such as regression, to test effects, we have tried to eliminate certain known hazards that tend to obscure impact.

3 Methodology

The methodology for this research was carefully developed with the substantive questions of the study in mind. As indicated in Chapter 1, the focus upon quality graduate education implied the use of multiple criteria of excellence. Because a number of technical considerations dictated the need for longitudinal data, information covering a 15-year period from 1958 through 1972 was used wherever possible.[1] This circumstance, together with the limited time frame in which the study was to be done, led to a heavy reliance on secondary analysis of existing data. As will be seen below, however, some additional data were collected during the course of the study. Another consideration was that any data used in the analyses had to be reliable and robust with respect to interinstitutional comparability. Finally, once the data were assembled, the selection of analytic techniques that would effectively untangle the causal relationships in the data was crucial. Specifically, methods were needed to detect the impact of Science Development funds in universities with varying overall budgets and to differentiate Science Development effects from general trends taking place in most universities during this time.

These considerations, then, constituted the frame of reference for developing a multifaceted research strategy that combined both qualitative and quantitative methods.

[1] For a fuller discussion of the values of longitudinal research, see David E. Drew, "The Potential Impact of Longitudinal Research on Decision Making in Higher Education," *Journal of Educational Data Processing*, Vol. 9, No. 1–2, 1971, pp. 30–35.

SITE VISITS

It was unnecessary to visit *all* Science Development institutions to get maximum benefit from the field trips since the diminishing returns would not have justified the costs. Nine of the recipient USD schools, one recipient of a SSD grant, and seven recipient DSD departments were visited.[2] These institutions were selected to include a variety of situations and thus to explore differing ways in which the grants were administered, unusual institutional contexts, and so forth.

In addition, five nonfunded institutions were visited for purposes of comparison. Given the qualitative nature of interviewing and the large number of variables operating, it would be pretentious to refer to these schools as "controls" in the rigorous statistical sense of that term. They were carefully chosen, however, to provide a suitable contrast with the recipient institutions. The goal was to select "borderline" institutions as controls; it was felt that the schools most like the funded institutions were those schools that had applied for grants but had been rejected.

Other factors contributed to the selection of site-visit institutions. One was the objective of examining a range of grants from those thought to be successful to those thought to be failures. Both public and private institutions were included; in light of the NSF emphasis on regional dispersion of the funds, a deliberate attempt was made to achieve a regional dispersion of site visits. Table 3-1 summarizes the distribution of site-visit institutions, with respect to control (public or private), region, and type of grant.

Since NSF considers the identities of institutions rejected for grants as confidential, it was decided early in the study not to reveal the names of any site-visit institutions in this report. This decision is consistent with the basic purposes of the study in that the site visits were used to generate general observations, conclusions, and recommendations; they were not intended as a school-by-school follow-up to assess how well grant funds had been spent.

The range of grants studied during the site visits is indicated by the following list of selected programs funded at the site-visit institutions:

Chemistry	Chemical engineering	Psychometrics
Physics	Mathematics	Statistics
Mechanical engineering	Social science	Ecology
Plant science	Geology	Materials science
Biology	Urban studies	Metallurgy
Microbiology	Information science	Animal science

[2] One institution that was visited received both a USD and a DSD grant, a fact that may explain some apparent discrepancies between the text and the accompanying tables.

22

TABLE 3-1 Type of Control and Regional Distribution of Site-Visit Institutions

	USD	Control	DSD and SSD	Control	Total
Public	4	2	5	2	13
Private	5	0	2	1	8
Northeast	1	1	3	0	5
Midwest	1	0	1	0	2
South	4	0	0	1	5
Southwest	2	0	0	0	2
West	1	1	3	2	7

Biochemistry	Computer science	Sociology
Biophysics	Economics	Aerospace engineering
Behavioral science	Political science	Molecular biology
Astronomy		

The site-visit teams to Science Development schools and control institutions were composed according to the following criteria: A member of the project staff, usually the director, was present on each visit. For visits to DSD institutions, the team was typically completed by one or two natural scientists who had participated in the preliminary NSF site visit during which the proposal was evaluated. The teams for the USD schools (and for controls) were larger, usually numbering four or five people. In addition to the project staff member, these teams commonly included one or more scientists who had been present on the initial visit to the school (or the subsequent visit when the institution applied for a supplementary extension of their funds). Moreover, each team included an educational administrator or a researcher with particular experience in higher education assessment. An attempt was made to include members of the study Advisory Panel or the National Board on Graduate Education on the site-visit teams.

While scheduling was kept flexible in order to adapt to unique institutional arrangements, the typical schedule was as follows. Prior to each site visit, the project staff member thoroughly analyzed the NSF grant file on that institution. The team met over breakfast on the day of the visit to discuss the particular issues to be explored. At an earlier date, each member of the team had been mailed information about the study and about the institution and its Science Development grant. In addition each had received a set of guidelines that provided the frame of reference for the visit. Some of the key questions in those guidelines included:

1. The overall goal of the University Science Development Program was to move universities into the category of "centers of science excellence." Do you feel that this was accomplished here?

2. What organizational factors seemed to be most related to specific areas of success: e.g., those departments which profited most from the grant? What implications does this have for decision making in future funding programs?

3. What organizational factors seemed to be related to departmental or institution-wide failures? How might this be avoided in future funding programs?

4. What unique assets and liabilities derived from the fact that the funding was given in this form of institutional support? Would this same level of funding have been more effective if given as project grants, on the one hand, or formula institutional grants on the other?

5. Was the school well prepared for the end of the grant? Have they been able to maintain the pace set during the funding? (This has particular implications with respect to state support of public institutions.)

6. Did the grant originate at the department level, or was the proposal initiated by the central administration? How is this related to success or failure?

7. Were the funds administered and controlled through the central administrations or were they essentially handled by the departments? How did this affect the success or failure?

8. What were the spillover effects on nonfunded departments?

9. Which kind of funding seemed to yield the greatest payoff: for personnel, equipment, or facilities? Do some of these yield short-term and some long-term payoffs?

10. Have there been any spillover effects on undergraduate education at the university?

11. What is the best way to build a quality science department? How has this been related in this institution to the receipt of the Science Development grant? How do the key factors vary depending on the size of the department?

12. Would more funds via a Science Development grant to the institution have made a significantly greater impact, or is there a limit to how much money can be used effectively at a given time?

Since several of these guidelines were inapplicable to DSD, SSD and control institutions, several additional questions, focusing on characteristics unique to those institutions, were explored in visits to those schools.

The visit began with a morning session during which the full team met with the president or chancellor of the institution, the institutional representative for the Science Development grant, and key provosts, deans, department chairpersons, and so forth. The goal was to discuss the overall impact of the grant on the institution with those people who had been central to the administration of the funds. In the afternoon the site-visit team dispersed, each team member visiting one or two departments to explore these issues in greater depth. One or two nonfunded departments at each institution were usually included. These nonfunded departments fell into two categories: those departments that had been included in early planning for the grant but did not receive funding (because of a university decision, a Foundation decision, or both) and departments that never had been considered for the Science Development grant but that might have experienced some spillover effects. During the visits to departments, department chairmen, faculty members, and graduate students were interviewed, and equipment and facilities acquired under Science Development support examined.

After the preliminary meeting, the site-visit team reconvened once or twice concluding with a wrap-up session at the end of the day. Subsequently, each member wrote a report on his/her observations emphasizing the guideline questions and focusing on his/her own area of expertise.

Each of the site visitors contributed much time and energy to this endeavor, and their work was extremely valuable to the successful completion of the study. Table 3-2 lists all those who joined a visit and prepared a report; their observations are reflected in Chapter 4.

QUANTITATIVE ANALYSES

The major focus of this study was on a series of quantitative analyses. The following sections describe some of the basic decisions that were made about sampling, the use of longitudinal data, and the techniques of analysis. In addition, the key input and control variables are listed, as are the dimensions of science excellence that were examined.

Sample Selection

In any large-scale evaluation study, selection of the experimental and control institutions is crucial. Early in the development of the design for this research, the notion of selecting a relatively small group of experimental and control institutions (say, ten of each) was rejected. We decided, instead, that the sample should include all USD recipients, many SSD and DSD recipients, and a sizable group of control institutions. Because of the many substantive and methodological objections that could be raised about any group of 20 or 30 institutions selected as controls, it was decided that the sample should comprise the entire group of doctorate-producing universities rated by Roose and Andersen in 1970.[3] This pool of 130 institutions included all USD and SSD recipients, 65 percent of the DSD recipients, and a substantial number of control institutions.

The rationale for this decision should be spelled out. In 1964 Allan Cartter of the American Council on Education (ACE) conducted a study in which he rated, field by field, the major doctorate-producing universities in the country in terms of the quality of the doctoral program and of the faculty.[4] The methodology was essentially peer review via a questionnaire survey. At that time, 106 universities met Cartter's criteria for inclusion:

[3] Kenneth D. Roose and Charles J. Andersen, *A Rating of Graduate Programs* (Washington, D.C.: American Council on Education, 1970).
[4] Allan M. Cartter, *An Assessment of Quality in Graduate Education* (Washington, D.C.: American Council on Education, 1966).

TABLE 3-2   Site Visitors

Dr. John Bardeen
University of Illinois

Dr. Dietrich H. Bodenstein
University of Virginia

Dr. Robert B. Brode
University of California, Berkeley

Dr. James W. Butcher
Michigan State University

Dr. William Cook
Colorado State College

Dr. Joan G. Creager
National Board on Graduate Education

Ms. Charlotte Davis
Washington International College

Dr. Joseph Doob
University of Illinois

Dr. David Drew
National Board on Graduate Education

Ms. Elaine El-Khawas
University Research Corporation

Dr. Hsu Fan
Purdue University

Ms. Ann Finkelstein
University Research Corporation

Dr. John Foster
Hampshire College

Dr. Robert Herman
General Motors Corporation

Dr. Joseph O. Herschfelder
University of Wisconsin, Madison

Dr. Walter Hibbard, Jr.
Owen-Corning Fiberglas Corporation

Ms. Margo Jackson
National Board on Graduate Education

Dr. Marion L. Jackson
University of Wisconsin, Madison

Dr. Robert M. Johnson
Florida State University

Dr. Lawrence Jones
University of Michigan

Dr. Charles V. Kidd
Association of American Universities

Dr. David Krogmann
Purdue University

Dr. Lyle Lanier
American Council on Education

Dr. Hans Laufer
University of Connecticut

Dr. Louis Levin
Texas Tech University

Dr. Frederick Lindvall
Retired, formerly with Deere & Co.

Dr. Ernest A. Lynton
University of Massachusetts

Dr. John Major
Massachusetts Institute of Technology

Dr. John Millett
Academy for Educational Development

Dr. Elliott Montroll
University of Rochester

Dr. Lincoln Moses
Stanford University

Dr. Norman H. Nachtreib
University of Chicago

Dr. Glenn Peterson
Memphis State University

Dr. Frank Putnam
Indiana University

Dr. Benton Rabinovitch
University of Washington

Dr. Meredith Runner
University of Colorado

Dr. Irving Shain
University of Wisconsin

Dr. Michael Useem
Harvard University

Dr. Stefan E. Warschawski
University of California, San Diego

Dr. James Warwick
University of Colorado

Dr. Heinz G. Wilsdorf
University of Virginia

In view of the decision to survey the major graduate schools, the simplest device was to include the institutions which formed the Council of Graduate Schools in the United States in 1961. To this group of 100, we added six universities which had granted 100 or more doctorates (spread over three or more fields) in the preceding decade. Thus, the 106 institutions include every university which averaged ten doctorates a year in the 1953–62 period.[5]

In 1969, ACE repeated this survey under the direction of Kenneth Roose and Charles Andersen; the number of institutions meeting the criteria had risen to 130. Since this was the most recent rigorous definition of this population, since we planned to work with the Cartter and the Roose–Andersen ratings, and since the Science Development program was at its peak in 1969, using these 130 schools as a base sample seemed to provide an optimal pool.[6] The universities in that group are listed in Table 3-3 as they originally appeared in Appendix B of the Roose–Andersen volume.

For the specific analyses reported in subsequent chapters, this total sample was subdivided further. Let us take, as an example, the field of mathematics. In some analyses (e.g., those relating to trends in Ph.D. production) the first group consists of all USD recipients that got funds for mathematics (among other fields). The second group consists of those institutions that received DSD or SSD grants for mathematics.[7] (DSD and

---

[5] *Ibid,* p. 10.

[6] The names of certain schools created some confusion among the research staff, usually because the school had changed names during the 15-year period covered in the analyses. Discovering such ambiguities in midstream, we decided to remove these few institutions from all analyses. The institutions were the University of California at San Francisco (Medical Center), Montana State University, and the University of Northern Colorado.

[7] There was an ongoing debate throughout the study over whether the Special Science Development recipients should be included with the USD or the DSD groups in the analyses. Shortly before the final computer runs the decision was made to include them with the DSD group. Since they had been grouped with the USD recipients in the preliminary runs, this decision led to some changes in the structure of the control groups. Thus, in the results reported in this volume, SSD recipients in fields other than the one under discussion have been included in the control groups where previously they had been excluded. Despite these changes in the experimental and control groups, the final analyses did not differ markedly from the preliminary runs.

The chief reason for the decision was that, even though the SSD grants were awarded on the basis of applications for the USD program, in actual practice the SSD grants more closely resembled the DSD awards in the following ways: (1) They averaged around $1 million, which is closer to the $600,000 average for the DSD awards than the $6 million average for the USD awards; (2) they involved only a few departments (and, in fact, it is hard to differentiate some of the institutions receiving SSD grants from institutions receiving several DSD grants); (3) they ran for three years and could not be extended with supplementary funds, in contrast to the USD grants that covered a five-year period, including a two-year supplementary grant; and (4) like the DSD grants but unlike the USD grants, they did not emphasize acquisition of equipment or construction of new facilities.

27

TABLE 3-3   Institutions Rated by Roose and Andersen

Adelphi University (N.Y.)
University of Alabama
American University (D.C.)
University of Arizona
Arizona State University
University of Arkansas
Auburn University (Ala.)
Baylor University (Tex.)
Boston University (Mass.)
Brandeis University (Mass.)
Brigham Young University (Utah)
Polytechnic Institute of Brooklyn (N.Y.)
Brown University (R.I.)
Bryn Mawr College (Pa.)
State University of New York at Buffalo
University of California, Berkeley
University of California, Davis
University of California, Los Angeles
University of California, Riverside
University of California, San Diego
University of California, San Francisco
  Medical Center
California Institute of Technology
Carnegie-Mellon University (Pa.)
Case Western Reserve University (Ohio)
Catholic University of America (D.C.)
University of Chicago (Ill.)
University of Cincinnati (Ohio)
Claremont University Center (Calif.)
Clark University (Mass.)
University of Colorado
Colorado State University
Columbia University (N.Y.)
University of Connecticut
Cornell University (N.Y.)
University of Delaware
University of Denver (Colo.)
Duke University (N.C.)
Emory University (Ga.)
University of Florida
Florida State University
Fordham University (N.Y.)
George Peabody College for Teachers
  (Tenn.)
George Washington University (D.C.)
Georgetown University (D.C.)
University of Georgia
Georgia Institute of Technology
Harvard University (Mass.)

University of Maryland
University of Massachusetts
University of Miami (Fla.)
University of Michigan
Michigan State University
University of Minnesota
University of Mississippi
University of Missouri
Montana State University
New York University
University of Nebraska
University of New Hampshire
University of New Mexico
New School for Social Research (N.Y.)
University of North Carolina at Chapel
  Hill
North Carolina State University at
  Raleigh
University of North Dakota
North Texas State University
University of Northern Colorado
Northwestern University (Ill.)
University of Notre Dame (Ind.)
Ohio University
Ohio State University
University of Oklahoma
Oklahoma State University
University of Oregon
Oregon State University
University of Pennsylvania
Pennsylvania State University
University of Pittsburgh (Pa.)
Princeton University (N.J.)
Purdue University (Ind.)
Rensselaer Polytechnic Institute (N.Y.)
Rice University (Texas)
University of Rochester (N.Y.)
Rockefeller University (N.Y.)
Rutgers University (N.J.)
St. John's University (N.Y.)
Saint Louis University (Mo.)
University of South Carolina
University of Southern California
Southern Illinois University
Stanford University (Calif.)
Stevens Institute of Technology (N.J.)
Syracuse University (N.Y.)
Temple University (Pa.)
University of Tennessee

TABLE 3-3 Continued

University of Hawaii	University of Texas
University of Houston (Texas)	Texas Agricultural and Mechanical
University of Illinois	University
Illinois Institute of Technology	Texas Tech University
Indiana University	Tufts University (Mass.)
Lawrence University Institute of Paper	Tulane University (La.)
Chemistry (Wisc.)	University of Utah
University of Iowa	Utah State University
Iowa State University	Vanderbilt University (Tenn.)
Johns Hopkins University (Md.)	University of Virginia
University of Kansas	Virginia Polytechnic Institute
Kansas State University	Washington University (Mo.)
University of Kentucky	University of Washington
Lehigh University (Pa.)	Washington State University
Louisiana State University	Wayne State University (Mich.)
University of Louisville (Ky.)	West Virginia University
Loyola University (Ill.)	University of Wisconsin
Massachusetts Institute of	University of Wyoming
Technology	Yale University (Conn.)
	Yeshiva University (N.Y.)

SSD recipients in fields other than mathematics were included in the analyses as control institutions.) The third, fourth, and fifth groups were control institutions. The "high controls" were those schools that ranked above the highest USD recipients in initial quality as defined by the Cartter rating of the quality of mathematics faculty, done in 1964, before any Science Development grants had been awarded. The "medium control" group were those institutions that were roughly equal to the USD recipients in initial quality; this group comes closest to the conventional notion of a control group. The "low controls" were those institutions that fell well below most of the USD recipients in initial quality. Only those institutions that had functioning, doctorate-producing mathematics departments at the time of both the Cartter and the Roose–Andersen surveys were included in this group. To summarize, the five major groups of institutions used in the analyses, and reported on in subsequent chapters, are:

Experimental groups:
    USD recipients
    DSD or SSD recipients

Control groups:
    High controls
    Medium controls
    Low controls

Two additional groups of control institutions were defined for a few of the analyses. One consists of those USD recipients that received funds only in fields other than mathematics. The other comprises those institutions that had no mathematics department in 1964 (at the time of the Cartter ratings) but had developed doctorate-producing mathematics departments at the time of the Roose–Andersen survey in 1969. Some of those institutions, such as The Rockefeller University, had developed outstanding departments in that short period of time, and it seemed inappropriate to lump them with the other "low controls": i.e., to define them arbitrarily as "low" simply because they had no mathematics department in 1964.

In a few of the analyses, the entire institution is used as the unit of study. In most cases, however, precise analysis required a field-by-field examination of the factors at work; in those cases, the groups defined above were broken out. For purposes of completing and clarifying this example, the specific institutions included in the five basic groups for the field of mathematics are listed in Appendix A. Of course, the definition of these groups differs for other fields (physics, chemistry, etc.); thus, the sample definition for each field is also given in Appendix A.

The Overall Science Quality Index

The concept of quality graduate education was constantly at the forefront as we made various methodological decisions. The central challenge was to develop operational definitions of a meaningful, but very vague, concept, *quality*. An additional problem was posed by the rather loose language used to describe institutional quality in the proposals creating the Science Development program. As noted earlier, the funding program was aimed at the 30 or so second-tier institutions that fell just below the top 20 in initial science quality. This language implies an unrealistic uniformity within the institution. That is, as any seasoned observer of higher education knows, a school with an outstanding mathematics department may have a poor chemistry department and a mediocre physics department; science quality is distributed unevenly across departments within the same institution. This was one of a number of reasons for conducting field-by-field analyses in this study.

In ranking institutions on the basis of their Cartter rating in a given field (say, mathematics), we found that the USD recipients were distributed widely, the greatest concentration being in the 20–50 ranks. As a measure of the degree to which the actions of the NSF administrators matched their rhetoric, a combined physical science measure was constructed; this was simply a computation of an institution's mean score as derived from the Cartter (quality of faculty) ratings in three fields: mathematics, physics, and chemistry. When the institutions were ranked on the basis of this measure (see Appendix A), the USD recipients were found to be clustered

30

more tightly within the 20–50 range. Thus, while intrainstitutional variability in departmental quality necessitated a heavy reliance on field-by-field analysis, the specially constructed overall science quality index tended to substantiate the notion that the USD recipients came from that tier of institutions just below the top 20.

Use of Longitudinal Data

To assess the impact of intervention aimed at change in higher education, longitudinal data are required. At a minimum, having a pretest measure on the criterion allows a researcher to test the hypothesis that differences in the measure after treatment do not simply reflect pre-existing differences. In addition, Campbell,[8] among others, has argued that a substantial period of time prior to the launching of the change program should be covered so that trends in the variables among experimental and control institutions prior to the awarding of funds can be taken into account. Unfortunately, not all previous research on the educational process has used a longitudinal design.

Perhaps the best-known, large-scale study of students is the Coleman report.[9] The impetus for this research was political. The 1964 Civil Rights Act required that the degree to which equal opportunity existed in the nation's elementary and secondary schools be assessed, with the added stipulation that the assessment be completed within two years. Although the findings proved provocative and produced an explosion of discussion and review, the fallout from that explosion contained many criticisms of the study attributable to the time constraint. To finish the study in the allotted period, Coleman and his associates had to assess changes that took place between, say, the first grade and the twelfth grade by examining groups of first-graders and twelfth-graders in a cross-sectional paradigm. The only way to draw accurate inferences about changes that take place during those school years and about the influence of various factors on these changes is to study the *same* group of students over a 12-year period. Obviously, Coleman and his associates, limited by possibly ill-considered legislative strictures, were unable to use a longitudinal design. In other contexts, however, where the need to find answers to problems is not so pressing or so politically loaded, such a design can and should be employed. The results of such research will usually be much less vulnerable to criticism.

[8] Donald T. Campbell, "Reforms as Experiments," *American Psychologist*, Vol. 24, 1969, pp. 409–29.
[9] James S. Coleman *et al.*, *Equality of Educational Opportunity* (Washington, D.C.: U.S. Government Printing Office, 1966).

As indicated earlier, our reliance in the present study on longitudinal data implied a reliance on existing data banks. The work reported in subsequent chapters was based on a careful selection of data from a number of federal and other data files; in most cases these provided trend information from 1958 through 1972.

Selection of Analytic Techniques

The specific methods used in the analyses will be described in greater detail in the appropriate sections. However, some general comments are in order here.

Obviously, the technique of analysis must vary with the nature of the question being explored. In some instances, simple descriptive statistics (e.g., percentages and means) were deemed satisfactory. Thus, for example, in examining the growth in faculty size of funded departments, one might begin with a simple cross tabulation of size, before, versus size, after. The next step might be to add a key control variable, such as public versus private (institutions). The next obvious step is to add an appropriate control group of comparable nonfunded institutions in which the same analysis has been carried out. The result would be a four-dimensional cross tabulation.

But these simple descriptive techniques are inadequate for probing causal relationships; more sophisticated multivariate methods are needed. For this project, we implemented a multiple regression package at the National Academy of Sciences computer facility, as well as several other multivariate techniques.

MEASURES OF SCIENCE QUALITY

Since multiple criteria were used to operationalize the concept of science quality, it seems appropriate at this juncture to briefly describe each of those indicators.

1. Perhaps the major thrust of the changes initiated under the Science Development program involved additions and modifications to the faculties of the funded departments. Thus, a key analysis in this study involved tracing the trends in faculty size in funded and control institutions.

2. To give an additional dimension to the above analysis (which focused simply on faculty size), an indicator of the research productivity of the faculty was included. Specifically, we conducted a field-by-field analysis of trends in publication rates by faculties of funded and of control departments in the most frequently cited journals in that field.

32

3. Several criteria focused on characteristics of graduate students. An initial analysis traced trends in total graduate enrollments and in first-year, full-time graduate enrollments.

4. A special survey was conducted to gather data that allowed comparison of the Graduate Record Examination scores of students entering funded and control institutions before and after the NSF program.

5. A similar comparison was made of the baccalaureate origins of these graduate students.

6. Since the rate of Ph.D. production is such a critical issue in national discussions of manpower needs (of Ph.D. unemployment and so forth), a very careful examination was made of the rate at which Ph.D.s were produced by funded and by control departments.

7. The previous measure is quantitative; a qualitative dimension was added by examining the characteristics of the academic institutions at which these Ph.D.s were employed in their first full-time job. (In the case of those Ph.D.s employed outside academia, we looked at trends in salaries.)

8. One goal of the funding program was institutional self-sufficiency in maintaining the momentum begun under the grant. In light of that concern and of the heavy emphasis on research productivity underlying the Science Development program, a key dependent variable was the amount of outside research support attracted to the department after funding; again, funded institutions were compared with control institutions.

INPUT AND CONTROL VARIABLES

The above list is a partial indication of the criteria used as reflections of science quality. In examining changes in those dependent variables and in assessing how these changes were related to the funding program, the pretest or earlier measures of these same variables were essential. In addition, several other factors had to be considered in assessing the effects of the Science Development program:

1. From a substantive and methodological point of view, it was vital to take into account whether the institution was public or private.

2. A given sum of money (say, $6 million over a period of six years) will have a dramatically different impact on an institution with an overall budget of $20 million than on one with a much larger budget. While no total institutional budget data were available which were comparable from school to school, we were fortunate to obtain an indicator of the annual federal support for science to the institution which met this criterion.

3. In examining items such as faculty publications, it was necessary to control for faculty size.

33

4. Similarly, in examining data on graduate student characteristics, it was necessary to control for enrollment size.

DATA ABOUT GRANTS

In addition to the input and output variables, extensive information about the grants was gathered and coded for use in the analyses. As will be seen, "dummy" variables were constructed to indicate whether or not each institution received a USD, SSD, or DSD grant or was a nonrecipient. In addition, detailed financial information was included in the analyses—on the amount of funds awarded under the categories of personnel, equipment, and facilities—thus allowing multivariate analyses of the unique impact of funds for each of these purposes.

4 Site Visits

The site visits provided a rich opportunity to observe the effects of the Science Development grants in a real setting. By examining the changes in faculty, graduate student enrollments, research, and so forth, at several funded (and nonfunded) universities, it was possible to add flesh to the statistical skeleton articulated in the analyses reported in subsequent chapters.

Moreover, these site visits can stand by themselves as a separate case study of the effects of Science Development. In this chapter, the general effects of the programs as observed in these visits are summarized, the side effects are discussed, and finally comments are made on a number of issues that arose in connection with the program. The methods used in conducting the visits have been described in detail in Chapter 3.

In addition, the methods used in drawing the conclusions reported in this chapter should be described. As indicated in Chapter 3, each site visitor produced a report giving his/her evaluations, usually running from three to five pages. These reports typically focused on the visitor's area of expertise and assessed the impact of the grant in terms of some of the guideline questions listed earlier. Following the completion of the last site visit, all reports—both by staff and by outside observers—were subjected to a content analysis. This analysis provided a profile of the general areas of agreement and disagreement among the site visitors with respect to the USD recipients, DSD recipients, control schools, and so forth. That content analysis formed the background for the development of the general observations reported below.

GENERAL EFFECTS OF THE GRANTS

After visiting a number of campuses, an observer is struck by certain obvious conclusions. The Science Development funds brought about numerous positive changes. In most cases they allowed the universities to take a giant step forward in their science capabilities. While some problems and liabilities were associated with the grants, the benefits greatly outweighed those detriments. In short, it is difficult to give $230 million to universities and do them much harm.

Though many universities showed significant improvement—in some cases a dramatic quantum leap—it would be inaccurate to say that there now are 50 centers of excellence where a decade ago there were only 20. More than the Science Development program is needed to create 50 institutions whose science excellence parallels that of Cal Tech and Berkeley.

Most administrators candidly admitted that they could not have absorbed much more money than the program provided in the five-year span. They would, however, have eagerly welcomed the continuation of funding at the same level over a longer time period. We heard numerous complaints from university officials about the erratic pattern of federal funding. One way to head off such dissatisfaction would be to establish programs on the basis of federal commitments for longer time periods; for instance, a program aimed at a ten-year funding period would have ensured greater acceleration in the sciences and would simultaneously have avoided some of the problems occurring when the crunch hit higher education. (These problems are discussed below.)

One statement frequently heard on the site visits was: "These funds allowed us to do things that no other source would have provided money for." It seems a unique experience for these institutions to be given vast sums of money targeted specifically toward their science departments but at the same time to be granted discretionary flexibility.

Sometimes these funds were used to establish new institutes, programs, or buildings that otherwise might not have existed. Frequently, they provided support for activities that would eventually have been launched anyway. But the key factor is that these Science Development funds greatly accelerated the pace of development, allowing universities to reach a point by 1970 that they might not otherwise have attained until 1980.

Another term continually used by the recipients of these funds was "catalyst." Clearly, these grants had a catalytic effect both on the development of the sciences and on the acquisition of additional funds. As noted earlier, NSF did not impose a technical matching requirement, but universities were expected to make significant financial contributions themselves. A number were able to use the grant as a basis for obtaining additional monies. For example, at one private university we heard about a meeting between the head of the university and the board of trustees before the school received a Science Development grant. The administrator indicated that an additional significant contribution from the university was required; by the end of the meeting, he had raised several million dollars from the board. In addition to this positive impact on the acquisition of "matching" funds, the necessity for the university to maintain the pace once the funding ended proved to be catalytic in acquiring funds further down the road. Some state universities, notably those that were judged more successful, found this requirement to be useful in increasing the level of their state support.

Thus, one can easily see a number of tangible positive effects of the program: brilliant new faculty acquired, graduate enrollment increased, buildings constructed, a telescope built, an exciting interdisciplinary institute established, and so forth. In some institutions, the progress was incredibly dramatic, particularly given the short time span involved, and some might argue that the progress of these schools alone would justify the program—particularly when compared with most federally funded activities. But some of the negative developments associated with the grants should be noted as well.

Some have maintained that Science Development was "the right program at the wrong time." It was launched in the mid-1960s, when all science activities were spiraling upward. Then in the late 1960s and early 1970s, when institutions were typically taking up their side of the bargain, the financial squeeze hit higher education: Federal funds were reduced, and the nation faced an "oversupply" of Ph.Ds in many fields. Some Science Development institutions found themselves overextended in the sciences; they had made a heavy commitment to a few major science fields that, because of NSF requirements, they felt obliged to maintain, occasionally at the expense of other fields. For example, in the eyes of some site-visit observers, a well-known program in agriculture at a major rural public university suffered because of this commitment to the basic sciences.

The problem seemed particularly acute for some public institutions that had extracted commitments from the state at the time the grant was awarded. Five or six years later, as the funding from Science Development was ending, they found that the state commitment in those fields was set in a budget that was not growing and often was shrinking. Thus, occasionally, Science Development distorted university support toward these funded fields when the crunch hit. It was interesting to note, though, that virtually all institutions involved made a sincere, and mostly successful, effort to live up to their commitment.

Another area hit particularly hard by the financial crisis was that of graduate student support. Frequently graduate students were attracted to the university by aid from Science Development funding and by the assumption that other resources would continue their support when the grant ended. Under more stringent financial conditions, however, support for graduate students was one of the first things to go.

A related criticism is that Science Development funded, and developed a commitment to, fields relevant in the mid-1960s, to the detriment of such fields as energy research and ecology that developed in the late 1960s and early 1970s. Given the Foundation's flexibility in redistributing funds within a department, it might have been advisable to structure the program so that it would have been easier for an institution to reallocate funds among departments as time passed.

Occasionally, the program had other negative consequences. In a few instances, the funds were given to institutions where a power struggle was under way, thus increasing the power of one or more of the participants and exacerbating the struggle.

It should be pointed out that the Foundation has a well-established policy of never interfering with the inner workings of a university. In light of this principle, Foundation officials have often deliberately stepped back from tricky situations and refused to take a stand. The irony, of course, is that any program that gives a university $6 million is by definition strongly affecting the inner workings of that institution. In a sense, that is one of the explicit goals of the program. So there is a basic contradiction involved here. The degree to which the Foundation—or any other federal agency— should become involved with the internal affairs of an institution is a problem that must be worked out independently in each specific case. Federal support of higher education institutions inevitably raises some thorny questions. Either of two extremes is equally distasteful: universities languishing without federal support vs. federal control of all university activities. Institutional aid is a mechanism to provide federal support while giving the institutions significant control over the funds. In contrast, project support substantially reduces the university's authority, in that the individually funded researcher can always threaten to take his money and go elsewhere.

One of the major benefits of the Science Development program was that it forced many institutions to plan in an organized fashion, as was often pointed out by people in universities or departments that were declined support. One is tempted to propose a scheme whereby a new national institutional funding program—one requiring extensive planning by the university—was loudly and widely proclaimed. The notion would be that, although no such program existed, the proclamation would lead universities into the kind of planning activity that would still yield immense payoffs for them.

38

ELEMENTS OF SUCCESS

When we compare extremely successful grants with others less so, certain distinguishing characteristics stand out. Perhaps the key factor is the strength of the central administration: Grants tended to be most successful at universities that had a strong and dynamic leader before, during, and after the grant; this was particularly true of USD grants. While this factor may be less important, even unimportant, in the case of project support, it is vital with respect to institutional aid.

Continuity in office is a point that should be underscored. Some upheavals were observed when an institutional leader who had been instrumental in acquiring the grant left prematurely (from the point of view of Science Development). Thus, not only a strong leader, but one committed to the university as well, is a vital element of success.[1]

Even though all concerned tried to use multiple objective criteria in awarding grants, it is clear in retrospect that one cannot underestimate the impact of a powerful personality. Whether a grant proposal originated with a department or with the central administration, one person usually played a driving role. For example, at one public institution, the chairman of the physics department prodded other department heads into writing their sections of the proposal. Thus, both in the preparation of proposals and in the successes (and occasional failures) of the grants, the presence of a strong individual was central.

It may be that the person receiving project support from the federal government becomes more committed to his research and less dependent on or committed to the institution, whereas the person who successfully administers a Science Development grant has a stronger vision of what the institution or department might become. The chief lesson to be learned from this comparison of successes and failures is that, in future funding programs, reliance should be placed on the person who has demonstrated *commitment to the institution*—not on one who will leave or who will favor a pet area.

Another component of success—and one associated with strong central leadership—is the existence at the outset of an overall development plan for the university. For many of the successful schools, the creation of a Science Development proposal amounted to carving out a section of an existing plan prepared as the result of extensive self-study; the Science Development funds contributed to an overall balanced effort. In addition,

[1] It appears that one by-product of the funding program was to elevate a number of natural scientists in the recipient departments to the higher levels of administration at their institutions. Occasionally, the head of the institution who greeted us on the site visits was a recently appointed scientist from a funded department.

these schools tended to be the ones that were best managed in general and as a result were relatively strong financially. Perhaps it is not surprising that in successful institutions that had these characteristics, comments about how the program had helped to strengthen nonfunded departments, to improve undergraduate education, and so forth, were most frequently heard.

CENTERS OF EXCELLENCE

When this program was launched, the key term—particularly in the political rhetoric—was centers of excellence, which was usually used in connection with the development of regional centers. The term assumed so much importance that an analysis of its implications is something more than a word game.

Both the term itself and the notion of regional distribution of funds had a dramatic political appeal that helped to persuade Congress and the public to fund the program—an advantage not to be underestimated, since decisions about science take place in an administrative and political environment.

The term also had a positive impact on the recipient institutions. People at the school and in the surrounding area were proud that their institution was slated to become a "center of excellence." Frequently, this improvement in image helped to attract matching funds and funds for continuing support.

On the other side of the coin, this phrase, particularly when combined with the notion of expanding the top 20 institutions to 50, may have resulted in the setting of goals too lofty for a program of this size. As noted earlier, while many institutions made major advances under this program, few appear to have caught up with the top 20.

In recognition of some of the liabilities of the phrase, NSF officials responsible for Science Development, notably Dr. Louis Levin, abandoned it midway through the program's history. But because of its early frequent use, the term stuck as a label for Science Development.

The notion of a regional center is attractive. An excellent university benefits the surrounding area; it is a provider of skilled manpower, a repository of knowledge, a source for consultation to business and industry. The top 20 institutions are, for the most part, clustered in the Northeast, the upper Midwest, and California. At first glance, the USD grants do not seem to have taken up the slack in the rest of the country in any uniform way. Some states received two or three grants, while many received none. Certainly, the awarding of three grants to the clustered universities in North Carolina helped establish a regional center of excellence among these combined "triangle" universities. But in another case it is difficult to see the value of a USD grant to an institution in a city that already had two outstanding universities. The grants in the Southwest and West tended to be distributed along the coast; except for one USD grant to an institution in Colorado, there was no funded institution (USD) in a vast region including the Plains or Rocky Mountain states.

However, many other factors besides regional impact played a role in the selection of funded institutions. In fact, there was a basic contradiction in the philosophy of Science Development program in that funding second-tier universities and disbursing the funds on a regional basis are somewhat contradictory. That is, the eligible universities were not distributed uniformly throughout the country. Thus, the pattern of the USD grants appears more reasonable when compared with the national pattern of eligible schools and of population centers.

USD VS. DSD GRANTS

The Departmental Science Development program was initiated after the primary USD program had been under way for some time. The major reason for its creation was to bolster selective departments in otherwise weak institutions, the notion being that these departments were ready to move to excellence while the institution as a whole was not. The range of subjects funded by the DSD grants was wider and more varied than in the USD grants. Moreover, DSD grants were given not only to departments in public and private universities but also to some primarily undergraduate institutions.

In addition to the greater diversity represented in the departmental grants, this subprogram was an excellent vehicle for generating truly interdisciplinary efforts. The site-visit teams observed some very success-ful institutes that had been made possible through DSD funds and were functioning superbly as interdisciplinary endeavors. It is intriguing to speculate why this subprogram was so effective at fostering interdisci-plinary work. Perhaps the larger size and the multidepartmental nature of the USD grants called for more administrative work and was thus less effective at stimulating interdisciplinary efforts.

With respect to the acquisition and implementation of DSD grants, the importance of a strong, charismatic leader was again evident. The site visits indicated that the more successful DSD grants developed under the direction of a particularly innovative department chairman or scholar. Perhaps this factor is related to the interdisciplinary thrust. That is, a charismatic leader may be able to create a new interdisciplinary effort through a DSD grant without becoming enmeshed in the bureaucratic interplay required by the larger USD grants.

41

Even though these funds were targeted for single departments, they still were considered by the Foundation, and by the recipient universities, to be institutional grants. In one notable case, they became the focal point of a dispute between a powerful department chairman and the central administration at a public institution. The Foundation, forced to take sides, felt that given the philosophy of the program, it had to support the central administration.

One weakness of funding a single department, in contrast with the broader USD support, is that peripheral, related substantive areas are not strengthened at the same time. For example, the researchers in one basic science department at a public institution located in a remote area complained that though their department had made dramatic strides, the weakness of related departments created a problem; this was compounded by their isolated location, which made collaboration with researchers in nearby universities impossible. In future funding programs limited to a single department, federal agencies should consider setting aside additional funds to bolster related fields at the same school.

EFFECTS ON NONFUNDED DEPARTMENTS

Studying the impact of the Science Development grant on nonfunded departments requires splitting this category into two groups: those that applied for funds and were rejected and those that never applied. Rarely did the former group indicate, after the fact, that they felt their rejection had been a Foundation mistake; indeed, in some cases, the rejection led the university to recognize a department's weakness and to attempt on its own to strengthen that area in addition to those that had been funded. For example, in the case of one major private institution, the Foundation indicated its willingness to support all of the proposed departments except mathematics. Forced to acknowledge the dismal national image of its math department, the institution (which had a highly successful experience under the grant) decided to rebuild the department and, during the period of the USD grant, poured substantial funds of its own into mathematics. Perhaps the story of the changes in that department is best reflected in the (full-time equivalent) faculty size before, during, and after the grant: from 11 to 4 and finally to 26. In short, the entire mathematics department was revamped as a direct result of the Foundation's decision that it did not possess the strength to move toward excellence under USD funding.

As another example, a department chairman in a public university whose application had been turned down when several other departments received USD funding commented that it was the best thing that had ever happened to his department. From that time on, he was able to plead poverty in his applications to other federal agencies and shortly landed another large grant that helped the department to advance.

Nonfunded departments in recipient institutions that had never applied for a grant (e.g., the humanities) had mixed experiences. In some cases, the generally increased affluence, stature, and momentum of the university had a positive spillover effect. For example, the chairman of the sociology department at a public university that received funds in the physical sciences felt that he had benefited indirectly from the USD grant in several ways. For one thing, the university, having developed the physical sciences, was now turning its attention to the social sciences. For another, the school's computer capability, built in support of the physical sciences, was useful to sociology as well. In other cases, nonrecipient departments felt resentful; this was manifested in the occasional complaint that those in the funded departments were receiving exorbitant salaries.

STRATEGIES FOR DEVELOPING STRONG DEPARTMENTS

As a by-product of this research, we explored the methods used by department chairmen and university presidents to develop strong departments. Certain patterns emerged during the site visits.

Most department chairmen felt that the way to achieve visibility in the academic firmament was to hire a few superstars. Three strategies were used to fill these distinguished professorships. First, some chairmen hired outstanding researchers from other universities.[2] Second, according to some observers, the department head hired a relatively mediocre researcher and labeled him a distinguished professor. Third, extremely able and promising junior faculty members were promoted and given all the support, equipment, and facilities they needed.

It is clear that the optimal strategy for department development varies from field to field. The chairman of a funded molecular biology department commented that his philosophy had been to hire only promising junior people because this field was new and did not have as many established stars as did other fields. Certainly, in some of the natural sciences, the development of a strong department requires a heavy investment in equipment and facilities, whereas in the social sciences or humanities, the focus is much more upon people.

[2] One of the issues surrounding the Science Development program, analyzed quantitatively in Chapter 5, is the degree to which the development of faculties in the funded institutions meant "stealing" good people from the top 20 and, in fact, from the other Science Development institutions.

NOTES ON PEER REVIEW

By structuring the site-visit teams as described in Chapter 3 and by including scientists who had made earlier visits to evaluate the proposals, this study continued the tradition of peer review. Thus, it is possible to comment on the adequacies of that system. The small size of the circle of scientists from which such groups are usually selected has been discussed by others; the existence of interlocking directorates and overlapping boards is indisputable. All the scientists who participated in the visits were able, hard-working, and cooperative, but as one staff member noted, virtually all were also white, male, and over 60, even though the study made a concerted effort to break that pattern. The risk in such a situation, of course, is that the range of opinions and assessments is likely to be limited.

One possible way to break the pattern is to provide opportunities for younger scientists to participate on site-visit teams in evaluating proposals, programs, and so forth. A junior faculty member might combine the necessary education and background with a freshness of perspective missing in the present situation. In this project and others, there is the risk that site visits will become occasions for polite, gentlemanly mutual praise. Many scientists and administrators—who often are meeting with colleagues whom they have known for some time—seem reluctant to ask difficult or piercing questions: e.g., about the deleterious effects of the funding.

OBSERVATIONS ABOUT NSF ADMINISTRATION OF THE PROGRAM

These site visits also provide an excellent opportunity for Monday morning quarterbacking: That is, the staff and board members on this study, having no connection with the NSF program, could assess objectively the adequacy of the Foundation's administration of this program.[3]

As part of the research for this study, the project director made a determined effort to discuss the issues involved with a number of former and current NSF officials who had been responsible for Science Development. One clear impression that emerged from these discussions was that these administrators were well chosen and are several cuts above those generally found in the government bureaucracy. Clearly, the Foundation viewed Science Development as a major innovative program and sought out the best possible scientists and administrators to manage it.

---

[3] The procedures and strategies followed by NSF in managing Science Development were described in Chapter 2.

Specific aspects of the NSF management of Science Development deserve both high and low marks.

Again and again in these visits, recipients of the funds paid great tribute to the *flexibility* of the NSF personnel in administering the grants. Repeatedly, one heard stories of how, when the crunch hit and the institution requested to transfer funds originally allocated for personnel into equipment, for example, or vice versa, their requests were approved with relative ease. Clearly, the Foundation had decided that the notion of institutional support implied a willingness to let the institutions manage the funds in the way that seemed to them most intelligent. It was common to hear a university administrator praise the Science Development bureaucrats as the best and most flexible he had encountered in years of dealing with Washington.

The perspicacity of the Foundation's judgments in making awards was noted both at funded and nonfunded institutions and departments. Rarely did it appear, in retrospect, that the Foundation should have given a grant to an institution that it had turned down; the same held true for departments. Almost inevitably, a reassessment of the judgment years later revealed that it had been on target, and university and departmental officials who had worked on the proposal would often admit as much to the site visitors spontaneously.

On the negative side, there is some evidence of interdepartmental jealousies within the Foundation that may have lessened an institution's chances of getting funding through another program. Apparently, the reasoning was, "They already got a big chunk of money from Science Development so we should distribute our funds elsewhere." A less explicit, but more bureaucratically meaningful, reason may be that the credit for progress probably would have gone to the larger Science Development grant; thus, there would have been less payoff to the managers of other departments. It is unclear how serious this problem was or what the solution is. Perhaps a greater emphasis on intraorganizational communication would help.

A more serious problem, which seems obvious in retrospect, is that the Foundation did not require enough from the recipient institutions in the way of evaluative reports on the effects of the funding. Though a few universities spontaneously provided such reports, with department-by-department evaluations, most did not, and it is virtually impossible to assess the impact of these funds by examining the NSF file on the institution. The Foundation did require progress reports annually and at the end of the grant; some schools were asked to submit additional reports. But typically these amounted to a brief text followed by the curriculum vitae of faculty who had been acquired under the grant. The relative lack of feedback from the funded universities about what was accomplished is unfortunate. Such feedback would have been extremely useful to NSF and, in the absence of a large evaluative study such as this one, would have provided information about the progress of the grant.

Dr. Louis Levin, a former key administrator of the program, noted in personal communications with the project director that the Foundation's aim was to minimize the amount of paperwork and administrative red tape for the recipient universities consistent with the general goals of the program. Nonetheless, requiring recipient faculty members and administrators to pause and assess the effects of the grant would have yielded a powerful payoff for relatively little effort on their part. Incidentally, Dr. Levin did initiate a survey of recipient institutions and departments that gathered detailed information on the distribution of funds and the number of personnel acquired under the grant. While this survey stopped short of an extensive evaluation, it provided very useful data.

MISCELLANEOUS OBSERVATIONS

It is intriguing to speculate about why the social sciences were not more heavily funded in this program. As noted in Chapter 2, some saw the DSD subprogram as a potential vehicle for strengthening the social sciences. A former administrator of the program commented that the Foundation had tried without success to encourage more social scientists to apply for both USD and DSD grants. In fact, it encouraged the social scientists in one private university that already had received a USD grant in the natural sciences to submit a second USD proposal in their area. Just after that proposal was submitted, however, the entire Science Development program was halted. One wonders whether the natural science community would have been in a better position to deal with the previously unforeseen environmental and energy crises—each of which has a social component— if the social sciences had been strengthened through the Science Development program.

Finally, the major focus of this program was understandably on research. But the lack of concern about the student, especially the undergraduate, on the part of the Foundation officials, the faculty members at the institution, and so forth, is deplorable. Ironically, those institutions that expressed the most concern for undergraduate education were the same institutions that seem to have made the most dramatic progress in developing their science capabilities at the graduate level.

5 Faculty Size and Mobility

In the eyes of many people, developing a high-quality science department means, in essence, hiring excellent faculty members. Thus, it seems appropriate to begin discussion of the quantitative analyses with faculty attributes, though these constituted only one of several indices used to operationalize science quality. Clearly, the first step was to look at the changes in faculty size that resulted from Science Development funding. In this chapter, the growth trends of faculty in Science Development departments are compared with trends in the departments of control institutions and of the control department, history.

An additional analysis was performed to see whether the changes observed represented a zero-sum or a non-zero-sum situation. That is, Science Development and similar programs have occasionally been criticized on the grounds that, from a national point of view there is no net gain in faculty quality because Science Development institutions improve largely by "stealing" talent from the top universities. The final section of this chapter reports on a special analysis conducted as a test of the hypotheses implicit in that criticism.

DATA SOURCES

Detailed information at the departmental level on university faculty is, unfortunately, not available for each year of the 15-year period used in this

47

study. Although such data have been collected for the National Faculty Directory during several recent years, data on the earlier years is lacking. The American Council on Education, in 1969 and again in 1972, conducted an extensive survey of a sample of the nation's faculty, but this source, too, failed to provide a full longitudinal tracing of the demographic information sought. Finally, one or two professional societies—notably the American Institute of Physics—have gathered information on faculty in one field with some regularity. The information yielded by this source, however, would not have provided a means to compare trends across fields or, more to the point, between science and the control field of history.

Thus, we sought a source that would cover time points from 1958 through 1972, give full national coverage, and yield information on faculty at the department level for the three science fields and the control field.

The data source that came closest to meeting all three criteria was the quadrennial *American Universities and Colleges*, a publication of the American Council on Education. This volume appeared four times during the 15-year period under consideration: 1958, 1962, 1966, and 1970. It gives a detailed description of each college and university in the country, including a breakdown, by department, of the faculty size.[1] For each department, the faculty is further categorized according to academic rank: instructor, assistant professor, associate professor, full professor, part time, and other.[2]

TRENDS IN FACULTY SIZE

Before comparing faculty growth at funded and at control institutions, it is instructive to examine the general trends at all universities during the time period under consideration. Table 5-1 shows the departmental faculty sizes

[1] The recent growth of branch campuses posed some problems in collecting these data. They were resolved as follows. In California and New York, it was usually easy to know which campus was meant. In other states only the main campus (e.g., the University of Wisconsin at Madison) was used for data on faculty size since it would be the one listed by Roose and Andersen as a major doctorate-producing institution. Occasionally, in collecting information from other sources, we were unable to sort out branch campus data from data pertaining to the main campus. Thus, for instance, in retrieving journal data from libraries, we encountered some periodicals that identified the author's affiliation as simply (for instance) "University of Wisconsin." Of necessity, such identifications were attributed to the main campus, in this example to the University of Wisconsin at Madison.

[2] To code consistently the information from *American Universities and Colleges,* some minor technical adjustments had to be made. A few institutions for which no data were reported had to be dropped from the analyses of faculty size. Occasionally, department names changed over the 15-year period. Sometimes this was a change in designation only; in other cases, it reflected an actual change in the composition of the department, requiring extrapolation on our part to maintain consistency.

TABLE 5-1   Overall Trends in Faculty Size, by Field (all major institutions)[a]

	No.	1958	1962	1966	1970
Mathematics	66	21.9	25.7	36.7	39.0
Physics	80	17.9	22.0	28.7	32.3
Chemistry	88	18.3	20.0	23.7	27.1
History	74	15.9	19.0	24.9	27.5

[a] Includes all departments rated by Cartter in each field, except those USD institutions not funded in that particular field.

for all institutions in each of the three science fields (physics, chemistry, and mathematics) and in the control field of history for the four time points for which data were available.[3] The same data are presented graphically in Figure 5-1. Note that the general trend in each field was a sharp increase thoughout the 1960s, an increase that had begun to taper by 1970.

Mathematics

In Table 5-2, the trends in faculty size in the field of mathematics are presented separately for each of the five institutional groups: USD recipients, DSD and SSD recipients, high controls, medium controls, and low controls. In addition, these data are reported separately for public and for private institutions. Basically, faculty sizes at the USD recipients increased dramatically, particularly in comparison with faculty growth at the medium controls, the most appropriate control group.

Further inspection reveals that this trend was evident in both the public and private sectors; in both sectors the USD recipients began with smaller faculties than the controls and finished with larger departments. Note that the mathematics departments in private institutions were much smaller than those departments in public institutions at each time point. Additional examination of the data revealed that the increase in USD-funded faculty sizes was most evident in those institutions with substantial overall federal science support, as contrasted with those with only moderate federal support for science.[4]

---

[3] In this table, and all others in this chapter, departmental size is computed by adding all full-time faculty categories.

[4] The distinction between "substantial" and "moderate" science support was made on the basis of data published by the government on the annual total federal support for all science activities in each university. All institutions that were above the median in total federal science support were classified as having substantial support; all institutions below the median were classified as having moderate support.

49

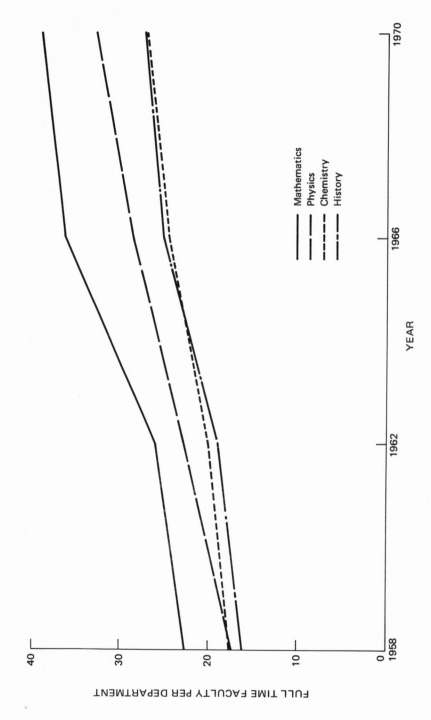

FIGURE 5-1 Overall trends in faculty size, by field (all major institutions).

YEAR

FULL TIME FACULTY PER DEPARTMENT

Mathematics
Physics
Chemistry
History

50

TABLE 5-2 **Departmental Faculty Sizes in Science Development and Control Institutions: Mathematics**

	No.	1958	1962	1966	1970
All Institutions					
USD recipients	15	20.4	24.3	37.8	42.2
DSD recipients	5	13.4	14.2	22.4	33.4
High controls	17	30.4	35.9	52.7	50.9
Medium controls	15	24.2	26.9	37.2	35.7
Low controls	16	14.0	17.9	23.2	28.8
Public Institutions					
USD recipients	9	22.0	27.9	44.3	50.6
DSD recipients	2	17.5	18.0	25.0	43.5
High controls	6	36.8	47.7	78.2	74.2
Medium controls	8	28.6	32.1	44.4	43.9
Low controls	10	19.0	22.7	29.7	37.9
Private Institutions					
USD recipients	6	18.0	18.8	28.0	29.7
DSD recipients	3	10.7	11.7	20.7	26.7
High controls	11	25.6	27.1	33.6	33.4
Medium controls	7	19.1	21.0	29.0	26.4
Low controls	6	5.7	10.0	12.3	13.7

Physics

Table 5-3 presents the data on faculty size for the field of physics. The trends in the growth of physics faculties at public and at private universities differ strikingly. In the public institutions, the USD recipients began in 1958 with significantly smaller faculties than the medium controls (18.1 versus 25.3). By 1970, apparently as result of Science Development funding, the situation had been reversed; the USD faculties (42.9) exceeded the medium controls (35.4). In the private institutions (where, once again, departments tended to be smaller), the USD recipients started out with larger faculty sizes than the medium controls and retained this advantage. Thus, Science Development funding seems to have had no effect on faculty size at these institutions.

Chemistry

Table 5-4 shows the data on faculty size for chemistry. Once again, the USD recipients began with smaller faculty sizes than the medium controls; but after funding, the situation was reversed. Further examination of the table reveals, however, that this trend was most apparent at public institutions; in private institutions, the USD recipients had larger faculties than the

TABLE 5-3 Departmental Faculty Sizes in Science Development and Control Institutions: Physics

	No.	1958	1962	1966	1970
All Institutions					
USD recipients	25	17.6	23.3	33.0	37.4
DSD recipients	9	9.3	12.7	17.7	24.1
High controls	14	33.8	39.4	45.3	48.9
Medium controls	18	19.4	21.9	28.3	29.7
Low controls	19	9.8	11.6	15.8	19.1
Public Institutions					
USD recipients	16	18.1	24.3	36.3	42.9
DSD recipients	6	9.2	12.2	17.5	27.0
High controls	4	31.3	37.5	46.0	53.3
Medium controls	8	25.3	27.6	34.4	35.4
Low controls	13	11.1	13.5	18.6	22.6
Private Institutions					
USD recipients	9	16.6	21.6	27.2	27.8
DSD recipients	3	9.7	13.7	18.0	18.3
High controls	10	35.3	40.4	45.0	46.8
Medium controls	10	14.7	17.3	23.5	25.1
Low controls	6	6.7	7.3	9.7	11.3

TABLE 5-4 Departmental Faculty Sizes in Science Development and Control Institutions: Chemistry

	No.	1958	1962	1966	1970
All Institutions					
USD recipients	22	18.0	20.4	26.5	31.3
DSD recipients	12	16.2	16.3	18.8	24.7
High controls	15	27.4	28.9	32.6	35.3
Medium controls	17	21.7	23.7	26.9	29.4
Low controls	24	11.9	13.4	15.8	18.0
Public Institutions					
USD recipients	13	18.9	21.6	30.0	35.7
DSD recipients	8	18.9	18.3	21.1	29.0
High controls	5	35.0	35.8	40.4	46.6
Medium controls	13	23.4	25.2	28.8	31.5
Low controls	13	13.5	14.9	17.8	21.5
Private Institutions					
USD recipients	9	16.8	18.6	21.4	24.9
DSD recipients	4	10.8	12.3	14.0	16.0
High controls	10	22.0	24.5	27.8	27.1
Medium controls	4	16.0	18.5	20.8	22.8
Low controls	11	10.1	11.6	13.4	13.9

TABLE 5-5 Departmental Faculty Sizes in Science Development and Control Institutions: History

	No.	1958	1962	1966	1970
All Institutions					
USD recipients	24	15.5	18.4	24.4	27.7
High controls	14	28.3	32.4	41.3	39.8
Medium controls	18	14.3	17.7	22.9	26.7
Low controls	18	9.8	12.2	16.8	20.3
Public Institutions					
USD recipients	14	16.2	19.5	27.4	32.2
High controls	4	27.5	30.8	49.8	54.3
Medium controls	10	17.8	21.5	29.1	33.8
Low controls	9	8.4	9.9	16.7	21.4
Private Institutions					
USD recipients	10	14.6	16.8	20.2	21.3
High controls	10	28.8	33.3	37.1	31.6
Medium controls	8	10.0	12.9	15.1	17.9
Low controls	9	11.2	14.6	17.0	19.2

medium controls at each time point but one (where the two groups were about equal).[5]

History

Table 5-5 presents the data on the control field of history. Note that although the typical department grew, the five groups of institutions retained their relative position throughout the time period. In the analyses of data for this control field, all USD recipients with rated history departments are included as the experimental group, but of course, no grants were given in history. In the private institutions, the trend differed slightly from that in the public institutions. The private USD recipients had somewhat larger history departments at each point in time than the controls, whereas in the public sector the situation was reversed.

Summary

Figures 5-2 to 5-5 graphically present the data on the USD recipients and the medium controls for all four fields. University Science Development

[5] Note that the sample selection procedures described in Chapter 3 yielded only four private institutions in the medium control group for chemistry. Thus, the data for this subgroup should be interpreted with extreme caution.

53

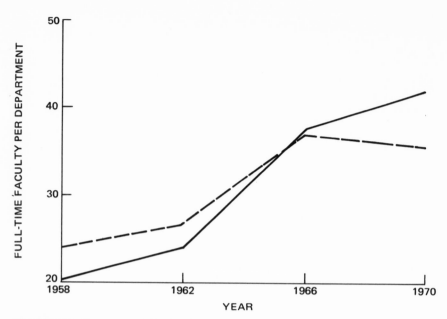

FIGURE 5-2 Departmental faculty sizes in science development and control institutions: mathematics.

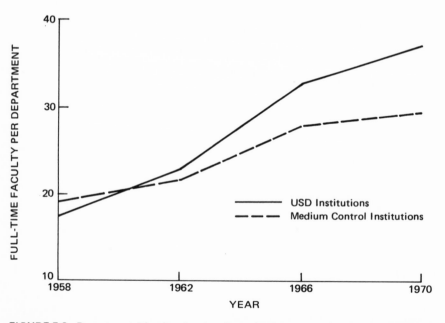

USD Institutions

Medium Control Institutions

FIGURE 5-3 Departmental faculty sizes in science development and control institutions: physics.

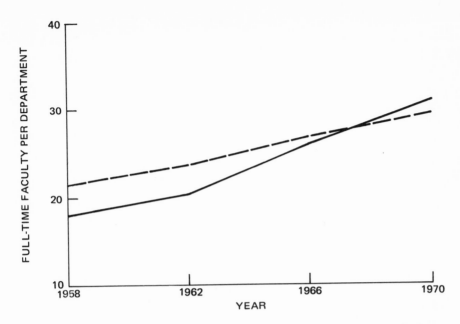

FIGURE 5-4 Departmental faculty sizes in science development and control institutions: chemistry.

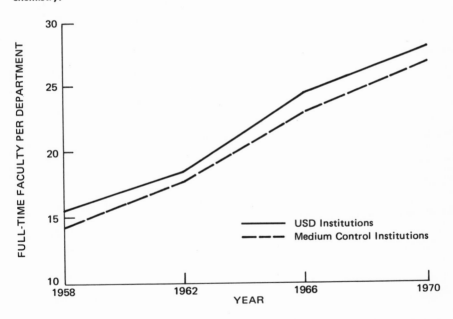

FIGURE 5-5 Departmental faculty sizes in science development and control institutions: history:

recipients in all three science fields had smaller faculties than the controls prior to funding and larger faculties afterward. This marked improvement on the part of the recipients did not occur in the control field of history, where no grants were awarded. The significant growth of Science Development recipients was greater in the public sector than in the private domain.

A Multivariate Analysis of Impact

The results presented above are essentially zero-order effects. They provide a basic descriptive profile of trends in faculty size in the experimental and control institutions without taking into account such related factors as total science funding to the institution. The next step was to examine the changes in these trends after these factors were controlled through use of a linear prediction model.[6]

The following method was used for this multivariate analysis. A number of dimensions from 1959 to 1961, which clearly preceded the Science Development program, were selected to represent those factors that were most likely to be related to subsequent faculty size. These dimensions became the independent variables for a series of multiple regression equations:

1. Total (departmental) graduate enrollment;
2. Departmental publication rate;
3. Departmental doctorate production;
4. Total federal science support for the institution.

Where possible, the variables were created by taking the average of the values for these years. Since the earliest year for which data on federal support for science were available was 1963, the figure for this year was used.

The analytical technique was as follows: The independent variables, taken together, were seen as representing the status of a given department with respect to certain key dimensions prior to funding. These variables were then systematically regressed on faculty size for 1962, 1966, and 1970. In Table 5-6, the results from these regressions are presented. The table includes not only the multiple correlations but also the regression coefficients for each independent variable in each equation.

Several mechanisms were used to test for, and isolate the effects of, the grant. First, a dummy variable was created, indicating whether or not a

[6] In this chapter, and in Chapters 6, 7, and 8, there will be slight differences between the samples used in the regression analyses and those used in the zero-order plots because a few schools for which significant data were missing had to be dropped from the former.

TABLE 5-6   Prediction of Faculty Sizes

	1962	1966	1970
Mathematics ($N = 65$)			
Multiple correlation	0.64	0.65	0.59
Regression coefficients[a]			
Doctorate production	0.18	−0.06	−0.13
Publication rates	0.08	0.27	0.25
Enrollments	0.41	0.46	0.42
Science funding to university	0.05	0.01	0.10
Partial correlations[b]			
Science development grant	0.04	0.12	0.24
All federal funds to department	0.24	0.35	0.38
Chemistry ($N = 87$)			
Multiple correlation	0.71	0.72	0.62
Regression coefficients[a]			
Doctorate production	0.12	0.41	0.05
Publication rates	0.39	0.09	0.36
Enrollments	0.26	0.25	0.29
Science funding to university	−0.04	−0.01	−0.06
Partial correlations[b]			
Science development grant	0.06	0.18	0.30
All federal funds to department	−0.02	0.06	0.33
Physics ($N = 82$)			
Multiple correlation	0.78	0.70	0.65
Regression coefficients[a]			
Doctorate production	0.10	−0.08	−0.30
Publication rates	0.21	0.00	0.28
Enrollments	0.42	0.61	0.42
Science funding to university	0.12	0.21	0.30
Partial correlations[b]			
Science development grant	0.06	0.11	0.25
All federal funds to department	0.20	0.40	0.20
History ($N = 71$)			
Multiple correlation	0.75	0.76	0.64
Regression coefficients[a]			
Doctorate production	−0.33	−0.26	−0.27
Publication rates	0.69	0.34	0.21
Enrollments	0.43	0.37	0.34
Science funding to university	0.03	0.38	0.41
Partial correlations[b]			
Science development grant	−0.05	−0.03	−0.01

[a] Regression coefficients are standardized.
[b] Partials controlled for the four variables above.

department got a grant. Then the partial correlation of this variable with faculty size, the criterion, was computed while controlling for all of the predictor variables. The size of this partial in a given year reflects the variation in faculty size for that year that can be attributed uniquely to the receipt of the Science Development grant. Each of these partials is presented in Table 5-6.

Data collected by the National Science Foundation yielded information about the total amount of federal support received by each department (including Science Development funds) in 1968. The partial correlations of this variable with faculty size also are included in Table 5-6. Differences between these measures and the grant partials provide a rough indication of the special impact of Science Development funds. [Comparison of these two partial correlations should be made with caution, however, since one of them (SD grant or not) actually is a partial point biserial correlation. That is, it is based upon a dichotomous variable, in contrast to the partial for departmental funds which is based upon a standard interval variable.]

As a further mechanism for examining the effects of Science Development, the equations developed in this analysis were used to generate predicted faculty sizes for each department for each year. These "expected" figures were then subtracted from the actual faculty size, yielding a residual score for each school for each year. Finally, these residual scores were averaged over the experimental and control groups and are plotted in Figure 5-6.

In other words, use of this linear model allowed us to predict faculty size in each school for each year on the basis of all key factors *but* Science Development funding. Differences in the predictive efficacy of the model between the experimental and control groups (as measured by the gap between these predicted rates and the actual faculty size) may be taken to indicate that the funding had an impact.[7]

This multivariate analysis strongly confirms that the Science Development program had a significant effect on recipient institutions, leading to an increase in the faculty sizes of the funded science departments. Both the partial correlations and the comparison of experimental and control residuals yield this conclusion. In all three fields, the growth in faculty size at the recipient institutions significantly outstrips what was predicted by the linear model based on conditions that existed prior to funding. For example, in 1970, the average USD chemistry department had 4.08 more members than expected, whereas the average medium control department had 0.35 more; in mathematics, there were 5.85 more faculty members than predicted at USD recipients, whereas the medium controls had 2.19 fewer

[7] Lincoln Moses and Donald Campbell made significant and valuable contributions to the development of this methodology.

than predicted; finally, in physics, the comparable figures are 5.38 more at USD institutions and 0.82 fewer at the medium controls.

ANALYSIS OF FACULTY MOBILITY

Critics of Science Development, both before and after the program was launched, claimed that a funding program of this nature would not benefit the nation because it would simply support the movement of scholars from one sector of the academic world to another, the assumption being that outstanding scientists would be "stolen" from the leading institutions by the USD recipients. These critics have claimed, for instance, that the only effect of Science Development on mathematics was to raise the salaries of the top 5 percent of mathematicians in the country. The question raised by such assertions is really whether Science Development funds had a non-zero-sum impact on the nation's pool of qualified scientists or whether, in fact, because of faculty movement, this was a zero-sum situation. This question is subject to empirical tests; that was the purpose of the analyses reported below.[8]

Whatever such an analysis reveals, some basic philosophical issues are involved here. Implicit in the criticism is the assumption that the movement of a faculty member from one school to another does not represent a net gain for the nation. But many would argue that it is in the nation's interest to build up the science capacity of certain geographically dispersed universities, even at the expense of the leading universities. The redistribution that results is not, in reality, a zero-sum situation but an overall advantage.

On another level, one can question whether one department of 150 physicists is equivalent in productive potential to three departments of 50 physicists each. This line of thought evokes the concept of "critical mass" as applied to faculty sizes: i.e., that a department must attain a certain minimum size to function effectively but that, beyond a certain point, size yields diminishing returns. Presumably, the critical mass threshold varies from field to field.

Having acknowledged these philosophical issues, however, the purpose of this section is not to debate them but to report on the empirical analyses that were conducted to assess the degree to which Science Development

---

[8] These faculty mobility analyses were conducted under the initial sampling assumptions that grouped SSD recipients with USD recipients. Subsequently, as noted in Chapter 3, a decision was made to recategorize the SSD recipients with the DSD recipients. Time constraints prevented the reanalysis of these data in accordance with these final (minor) sampling modifications. Consequently, the institutional sample sizes in this analysis differ slightly from those in other analyses reported in this volume.

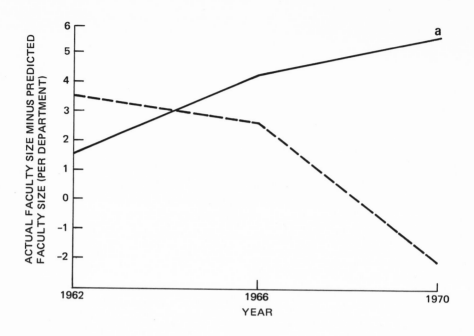

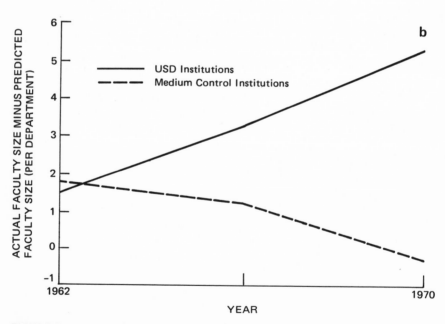

FIGURE 5-6 Residual analysis of departmental faculty sizes: (a) mathematics, (b) physics, (c) chemistry, (d) history.

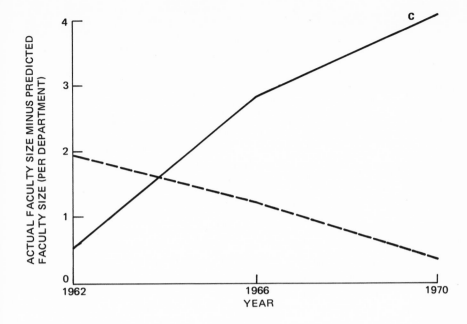

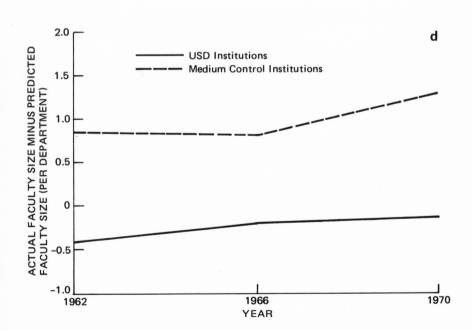

61

faculties were developed by "robbing" the leading institutions (or other Science Development schools).

The analyses of faculty mobility were limited to one field, physics, for a variety of reasons. First, of all the fields funded by Science Development, physics received the largest amount of money. In addition, detailed data on departmental membership were available on a year-by-year basis for physics. As mentioned earlier, the American Institute of Physics regularly collects such information.

The basic research design was as follows. The source school of each senior faculty member appointed to a USD school from 1965 to 1971 was identified. (Source school means the institution at which the faculty member previously held a position.) The patterns thus traced were then compared with the patterns for senior faculty members at the medium control institutions. Finally, as a further control, the entire analysis was repeated for the period 1959–1965. Each of these steps is described in more detail below.

The notion of "robbery" inherent in the criticism under investigation obviously applies only to senior faculty, notably "stars." Few would categorize the movement of a graduating Ph.D. to a junior faculty position at a Science Development institution as a case of "stealing." Consequently, of the total physics faculty at a Science Development or medium control institution, the "eligible" ones were those listed in the *Directory of Physics and Astronomy Faculties* as (1) chairman, (2) dean (or some other administrative title), (3) professor, (4) associate professor, (5) assistant professor, (6) on leave. Excluded were faculty members with the titles of (1) adjunct professor, (2) visiting professor, (3) lecturer, (4) instructor, (5) professor emeritus, (6) postdoctoral or research fellow. In addition to meeting our theoretical goals, this operational definition of senior faculty was practical in that all schools listed all our "included" titles in the directory, but not all of them listed the titles we were excluding. By examining the rosters of physics faculties at the USD physics recipients and medium controls, we were able to arrive at a count of the "eligible," i.e., senior, faculty.

The next step was to determine how many of those eligible faculty members represented new appointments during the period of Science Development funding. By comparing these 1971 (i.e., postfunding) lists with the 1965 (i.e., prefunding) directory, we were able to determine which of the eligible faculty represented new appointments at USD-funded and medium control institutions. (Because the comparison of the percentages of new appointments at USD and at control institutions was itself an interesting analysis, it is discussed below.) The sample under consideration now had been reduced to those faculty members representing new appointments in both experimental and control schools. The final sample

62

consisted of that subset of the new faculty members who were listed in *American Men and Women of Science* and whose previous jobs could therefore be identified.[9] Before we discuss the results of this analysis, a review of the terms used and their associated operational definitions may be useful:

Eligible Faculty   Senior physics faculty members listed as chairman, dean, professor, associate professor, assistant professor, on leave.

New Appointments   Those 1971 faculty members who were not at the same institution in 1965, or those 1965 faculty members who were not at the same school in 1959.

Experimental Schools   Those institutions receiving USD or SSD grants for physics.

Control Schools   The medium control group of institutions for physics.

Experimental Time Period   1965–1971.

Control Time Period   1959–1965.

Current Institution   The institution at which the faculty member was employed in 1971 (or in the case of the control time period, the institution at which the faculty member was employed in 1965).

Source School   The institution that the faculty member left to take a position at the current institution.

Table 5-7 presents data on the number of eligible faculty in 1959, 1965, and 1971 and of these the number who were new appointments as of 1965 and 1971. The data are presented for all institutions, public institutions only, and private institutions only. By subtracting the 1965 from the 1971 faculty sizes (and the 1959 from the 1965 faculty sizes), we can obtain an indication of how many of these new appointments represented replacements and how many represented an increase in faculty size. These figures, as well, are included in Table 5-7.

---

[9] Some minor technical decisions should be noted here. Consistent with our reason for limiting the analysis to senior faculty members, the new faculty members included in the sample had to hold a senior position at both the old and the new institution. An exception to the above rule was made if the new faculty member was a Ph.D. who had worked for three or more years at his previous institution. This exception allowed us to include some experienced senior researchers who conducted their work in high-level professional positions that at some laboratories (e.g., the Plasma Physics Lab at Princeton) happened to carry a title like Research Associate.

The control time period (1959–1965) was constructed so that the interval (six years) would match that of the experimental time period. Our data collection procedures were such that we would miss scholars who had moved twice within either time frame (1960–1964, 1966–1970), but who were at the same institution in a "before" and an "after" year.

The rare scholar who held a joint appointment at a recipient institution and at a source school was counted as one half in each category.

TABLE 5-7 New Senior Faculty Appointments at Science Development and Control Institutions: Physics

Group	No. Schools	Eligible Faculty/Dep.			New Appointments/Dep.		New Appointments for Expansion/Dep.	
		1959	1965	1971	1965	1971	1965[a]	1971[b]
USD schools	26	17.2	28.1	37.7	15.1	17.0	10.9	9.6
Public	17	17.9	30.9	43.1	16.6	20.1	13.0	12.2
Private	9	15.7	22.8	27.3	12.2	11.2	7.1	4.5
Medium control schools	13	19.3	27.5	30.8	13.5	10.2	8.2	3.3
Public	6	25.8	36.7	40.7	18.8	11.1	10.9	4.0
Private	7	13.7	19.6	22.4	9.0	9.1	5.9	2.8

[a] Eligible faculty (1965) minus eligible faculty (1959).
[b] Eligible faculty (1971) minus eligible faculty (1965).

64

Some of the new appointments could not be located in *American Men and Women of Science,* presumably relatively junior scholars and foreign scientists. For example, of the 443 new appointments to USD schools from 1965 to 1971, 94 were not listed. Of the remaining 349, 109.5 had been senior faculty members at another institution. Presumably, the other 240 fell into one of the following categories: (1) new Ph.D.s, (2) foreign scholars, (3) research associates and postdoctoral fellows; or recruits from (4) private industry, (5) private or semiprivate research organizations (e.g., Brookhaven and the Institute for Advanced Study), and (6) government.

The central analysis, of course, involved comparing the source schools of the senior scientists who had moved to a target university (recipient or medium control institutions). Table 5-8 presents the results of that analysis. There, the origins of new appointees to both USD and control schools in both time periods are presented for all institutions, as well as for public and private institutions only. The source schools were divided into seven categories:

1. USD and SSD recipients in physics;
2. Other USD recipients;
3. DSD physics recipients
4. High controls;
5. Medium controls;
6. Low controls;
7. Other schools.

The data in Tables 5-7 and 5-8 taken together present a complete picture of the sources of all senior faculty who moved to USD and control institutions during each of the two time periods. In short, they reveal the mobility of senior faculty in physics at these institutions during the period of Science Development and during a comparable time period before the program was launched.

Some obvious conclusions may be drawn. Prior to funding, USD and medium control schools were acquiring new senior faculty at about the same rate. After funding, the rate at the Science Development institutions remained the same, while the rate at the medium controls dropped. In short, Science Development funds merely allowed the recipient institutions to maintain the pace they had set between 1959 and 1965, whereas the competition slowed down.

These data do not support the criticism that the USD institutions developed their science capability at the cost of the high controls, or of any other group of institutions for that matter. If anything, the recipient institutions acquired faculty that might otherwise have gone to the medium controls—a reasonable outcome for such a funding program. (It is more

TABLE 5-8 Source Schools of Senior Faculty at Science Development and Control Institutions: Physics

Source Schools	No. Schools	1959 to 1965 USD No.	USD %	Medium No.	Medium %	1965 to 1971 USD No.	USD %	Medium No.	Medium %
All Institutions									
Total	—	96	24.4	36	20.5	109.5	24.7	31	23.3
USD funded in physics	26	14	14.6	10	27.8	16	14.6	7	22.6
USD nonfunded in physics	7	4	4.2	1	2.8	3	2.7	0	0.0
DSD in physics	6	1	1.0	0	0.0	2	1.9	0	0.0
High control group	14	40	41.7	17	47.2	57.5	52.5	11	35.5
Medium control group	13	8	8.3	2	5.6	7	6.4	3	9.7
Low control group	18	3	3.1	2	5.6	2	1.9	0	0.0
"Other" American colleges and universities	—	26	27.1	4	11.1	22	20.1	10	32.2
Public Institutions									
Total	—	70	24.7	18	15.9	84.5	24.7	18	26.1
USD funded in physics	17	10	14.3	4	22.2	13	15.4	4	22.2
USD nonfunded in physics	7	3	4.3	0	0.0	2	2.4	0	0.0
DSD in physics	6	1	1.4	0	0.0	1	1.1	0	0.0
High control group	14	32	45.7	8	44.4	44.5	52.7	5	27.8
Medium control group	13	7	10.0	1	5.6	5	5.9	1	5.6
Low control group	18	3	4.3	1	5.6	2	2.4	0	0.0
"Other" American colleges and universities	—	14	20.0	4	22.2	17	20.1	8	44.4
Private Institutions									
Total	—	26	23.6	18	28.6	25	24.8	13	20.3
USD funded in physics	9	4	15.4	6	33.3	3	12.0	3	23.1
USD nonfunded in physics	7	1	3.8	1	5.6	1	4.0	0	0.0
DSD in physics	6	0	0.0	0	0.0	1	4.0	0	0.0
High control group	14	8	30.8	9	50.0	13	52.0	6	46.2
Medium control group	13	1	3.8	1	5.6	2	8.0	2	15.4
Low control group	18	0	0.0	1	5.6	0	0.0	0	0.0
"Other" American colleges and universities	—	12	46.2	0	0.0	5	20.0	2	15.4

likely, given the trends in these data, that if the Science Development schools had not hired these new faculty members under funding, the control schools would not have acquired them either.) Most discussions of the "robbing" notion emphasize that the leading institutions lose top talent. These data reveal that, at least in the field of physics, they lost less senior talent overall during the funding period than before; the people leaving the leading institutions, however, were somewhat more likely to go to Science Development institutions than to their competitors. Given the large department sizes of the leading institutions, the defections in either time period were relatively trivial.

Further examination of these data reveals that any advantage that the Science Development institutions may have enjoyed over the controls in the "after-funding" period was limited entirely to the public sector. With respect to acquiring new senior faculty, trends at the private recipient institutions more closely followed those at the medium controls than those at the public recipient institutions. The finding is intriguing inasmuch as Science Development funds per physics department for personnel were roughly the same in the public and in the private sector.

The explanation for the advantage of public recipient institutions over other public institutions was suggested in the site visits, which revealed that public institutions used Science Development funds to hire new faculty, while at the same time extracting a commitment from the state to retain those faculty members once the funding ended.

A more tantalizing question is why the private recipient institutions, having roughly the same amount of money per department for personnel as the public recipients did not grow at a greater rate during the period of funding. As Table 5-1 indicates, in 1971, the number of new appointments for expansion in the private recipients was 4.5, compared with 2.8 for the controls—hardly a striking difference. The explanation may be that during the early 1970s, the recipient private institutions, faced with the financial crunch in higher education and finding it necessary to slow down their faculty growth, used their Science Development money as replacement funds in the funded departments, diverting institutional funds into other departments.

Taking a closer look at the high controls—i.e., the leading physics departments—we find that, in 1965, 40 of the 96 new appointments to USD schools came from these top departments, whereas after funding 57.5 of 109.5 were drawn from this group. This represents a small increase of roughly one extra faculty member "stolen" from each high control school over a seven-year period. In contrast, the medium control institutions acquired 17 out of 36 new appointments from the leading institutions in 1965; in 1971 they acquired 11 out of 31.

In short, the evidence refutes the criticism that the USD recipients

67

developed their science faculties by robbing the leading institutions. There is, however, one rather different way in which the leading physics departments may have suffered as a result of Science Development funding. It may be that the funding strengthened the recipient institutions to the point that they were less likely to experience defections. In short, the effect of the funding may have been to reduce the stealing of faculty members *by* the leading institutions.

6 Effects on Faculty Productivity

However important an indicator of Science Development's impact the increased size of university science faculties may be, the constant focus upon quality—in the program itself and in this evaluative study—made it necessary to look at the research productivity of these scientists.[1] The publication records of scientists from funded and from control institutions in the leading journals of their field was the measure of research productivity. This chapter reports the results of our analyses. Appendix B describes the methods used to select the key journals in each field.

In recent years an increasing amount of the work done in the history and sociology of science has centered on the analysis of publication and citation rates. Publication rates are a straightforward index of productivity; citation rates indicate the impact of an author's publications on professional colleagues. Studies of these two indices have yielded new knowledge not only about factors related to scientific productivity but also about patterns of communication within the sciences.

In a 1966 assessment of the strengths and weaknesses of the standard

---

[1] The other major function of a university professor—many would say the dominant function—is to teach. The unfortunate reality is, however, that there currently exists no valid measure of teaching performance that could be used to compare professors across schools; i.e. which has interinstitutional comparability. In addition, of course, the philosophical thrust of the Science Development program emphasized research productivity heavily. For better or worse, relatively little concern was given to teaching either at the graduate or the undergraduate level.

citation measure, Bayer and Folger[2] found that the measure correlated significantly with departmental prestige. Since then, Jonathan and Steven Cole[3] have carried out a series of studies in this area, relying heavily on data produced by a leading commercial firm, the Institute for Scientific Information, Inc., in Philadelphia; some of the analyses reported here also drew on data from ISI.

In one notable study, the Coles[4] argued that the citation pattern in science indicates that each field is dominated by a relatively small elite who make the major discoveries and who are frequently cited by others. This argument stands in contrast to the so-called Ortega hypothesis that progress in science is built on the efforts of a large number of lesser known researchers. Consistent with the Coles, Diana Crane maintains that scientific progress takes place in a social structure characterized by a small elite (the "invisible college") that plays a key role in the communication of knowledge.[5]

Similarly, Derek DeSola Price has advanced the thesis that each scientific field has an "in" group whose thinking and research dominate.[6] His work has led him to conclude that "there is a reasonably good correlation between the eminence of a scientist and his productivity of papers."[7] In the same book, he discusses some of the implications of Lotka's findings that the rate of production of papers by authors is an inverse square function: That is, for every 100 scholars producing a single paper, 25 produce two papers, 11 produce three, and so forth.

While these arguments are made in terms of individual scientists, not departments, they are pertinent to this assessment of a funding program based on the principle that the number of centers of science excellence should be radically increased.

The short time that intervened between Science Development funding

[2] Alan Bayer and John Folger, "Some Correlates of a Citation Measure of Productivity in Science," *Sociology of Education*, Vol. 39 (1966) pp. 381–390.
[3] Jonathan R. Cole and Stephen Cole, "Scientific Output and Recognition: A Study in the Operation of the Reward System in Science," *American Sociological Review*, Vol. 32 (1967) pp. 377–390; "Measuring the Quality of Sociological Research: Problems in the Use of the Science Citation Index," *American Sociologist*, Vol. 6 (1971) pp. 23–30; "The Ortega Hypothesis," *Science*, Vol. 178 (1972) pp. 368–375; *Social Stratification in Science* (Chicago: University of Chicago Press, 1974).
[4] Cole and Cole, op. cit., 1972.
[5] Diana Crane, *Invisible Colleges: Diffusion of Knowledge in Scientific Communities* (Chicago: University of Chicago Press, 1972).
[6] Derek J. de Solla Price, Donald deB. Beaver, "Collaboration in an Invisible College," *American Psychologist*, Vol. 21 (1966) pp. 1011–1018.
[7] Derek J. de Solla Price, *Little Science, Big Science* (New York: Columbia University Press, 1963) p. 40.

and this evaluation study effectively ruled out the use of citations as an impact measure. Citation rates were used, however, as the basic criterion for selecting the journals used in the productivity analyses. That is, in view of the focus on quality in this research, we felt it would be a mistake to analyze productivity simply by looking at publication in the full array of scientific journals; rather, it made more sense to look at publications in the leading, most often cited journals in the field. The use of citation rates as a proxy for quality (whether of individuals, departments, or journals) is a notion that has been endorsed by the Coles, Kenneth Clark,[8] and Bayer and Folger.[9] While there are important technical differences between the methods used by this study and those employed by Inhaber, it should be noted that his study of physics journals also relied on citation rates provided by ISI to select key journals.[10] Among the technical differences: In the current research, foreign language journals were eliminated, and multifield journals retained; Inhaber followed the opposite route.

A number of researchers have found not only that the publication rates and the citation rates of scientists are closely correlated with each other but also that each is closely correlated with other measures of quality. For example, in a study relevant to this evaluation of Science Development, Hagstrom[11] used data drawn primarily from a questionnaire administered to a large sample of scientists to analyze the correlates of departmental excellence, as measured by Cartter. Hagstrom found that his publication measure (geometric mean per department) and his citation measure were about equally highly correlated with departmental quality, the correlations for publication being slightly higher than those for citations.

After tracing the publication careers of a sample of scientists, the Coles concluded that there is a high correlation between citations and publications. Those scientists whose early works are heavily cited tend subsequently to publish more than do their colleagues. According to the Coles, "these findings suggest that when a scientist's work is used by his colleagues he is encouraged to continue doing research and that when a scientist's work is ignored, his productivity will tail off."[12] They also noted that this correlation between quantity and quality is stronger in the nation's top departments than in the mediocre ones.

[8] Kenneth Clark, *American Psychologists: A Survey of a Growing Profession,* (Washington, D.C.: American Psychological Association, 1957).
[9] Bayer and Folger, op. cit., 1966.
[10] Herbert Inhaber, "Is There a Pecking Order in Physics," *Physics Today,* Vol. 27, May, 1974, pp. 39–43.
[11] Warren Hagstrom, "Inputs, Outputs, and the Prestige of Science Departments," *Sociology of Education,* Vol. 44 (1971) pp. 375–397.
[12] Cole and Cole, op. cit., 1967, p. 389.

Thus, a growing body of empirical research on the sociology of science justifies the use of citation rates as a mechanism for selecting journals.[13] This same body of literature supports the notion that faculty productivity, as indicated by rate of publication in those same leading journals, can serve as a key indicator of quality, one that would correlate highly with numerous other measures of individual and departmental excellence.

As indicated earlier, in studying faculty productivity, we faced a time-lag problem. That is, the impact of Science Development grants on citation rates could not be expected to become evident until some time after the study was completed. The most active years for initiating Science Development grants were 1967 and 1968. Allowing at least a year for new faculty to be hired and several more years for work conducted under the grant to be written up and accepted for journal publication, it was just barely possible to detect effects upon publication rates; clearly, then, even more time is required for a published article to have an effect on the work of others, as reflected in citations to the article. Thus, it was necessary to look at publication rates rather than citation rates. But we did consider citation rates in selecting the journals to be used in the publication analyses.

The basic plan in this productivity analysis was to compare faculty at funded institutions with those at control institutions in terms of their publication rates from 1958 to 1972. Consistent with our continuing emphasis upon quality, however, only the best journals in the field were considered. If the faculty at Science Development schools were found to be publishing more (or less) in these key journals, this development would be much more significant than if they seemed to be gaining (or losing out) in relatively unknown, less selective journals. Moreover, restricting the set of journals to be analyzed is feasible in that the great preponderance of citations are made to these leading journals. For example, although the analyses for physics were limited to 20 journals, those journals accounted for 77 percent of all citations in the field. Finally, keeping the number of journals to be searched fairly small was a matter of practicality, given limitations of time and staff.

Once the key journals in physics, chemistry, mathematics, and history had been selected, as described in Appendix B, the next task was to compare the rate at which faculty from funded and from control institutions

---

[13] Citation measures have sometimes been criticized, usually on the following grounds: they fail to differentiate between favorable and unfavorable citations. Frequently, researchers attempt to generate a "halo" effect by citing the major names in their field rather than the lesser-known people whose work may actually be more directly linked to their own. Some profound work that has had a powerful influence on all subsequent research is so taken for granted that scientists often do not bother to cite it.

Use of the ISI citation file involves additional technical problems. For example, because of the structure of those files, work by two scientists with the same last name and first initial is indistinguishable.

published in these journals during the period 1958 through 1972. The techniques involved both data from magnetic tape provided by ISI and data retrieved clerically from journals in libraries.

The ISI data were available for the three science fields for the period 1965–1972. The Institute for Scientific Information retrieves considerable information about the author, title, and so forth, of each journal article published in each significant science journal every year. From these basic data, several files are developed: a source file, a citation file, and the one most relevant to this study, a "corporate index" file, which records for each source article the institutional affiliation (or "corporate address") of the author. A corporate address is entered into the file just once for each article even if more than one of the authors came from that institution. The file is, of course, sorted by corporate address. Thus, by categorizing the corporate addresses in terms of the recipient and control groups for the study, we were able to count the total number of articles published in influential journals each year by faculty in each group of institutions. This count constituted our basic measure.

As was pointed out earlier, the ISI corporate address file covered only the 1965–1972 period; earlier data (1958–1964) had to be collected by going through journals in libraries. To assure strict continuity, library retrieval was carried out according to rules conforming precisely to the somewhat idiosyncratic strategies used by ISI.[14]

A special problem in definition was posed by the wide variety of institutes and research centers with which scientific researchers are associated and which they give as their corporate address. Though specific decisions had to be made in each case, our basic criterion was as follows: If a research center was an integral part of a university, the university was "credited" with the article; those research centers which may have been in the same town as the university but were privately owned or not directly affiliated with the university were not counted.[15]

[14] Later, it was found that the two procedures differed in minor ways that would explain any slight gaps between publication rates in 1964 and in 1965. (How minor these differences were is reflected in the general continuity and smoothness of the curve from 1964 to 1965; in no case is there any sharp discontinuity.) Although ISI never repeats a corporate address for an institution, the firm's definition of corporate address is somewhat unusual in that, if two researchers from different departments in the same institution publish an article, it will probably be listed under two corporate addresses, since frequently (but not always) ISI includes the department as part of the corporate address. In those rare instances where this was the case, the library researchers would have credited the institution only once. Our belated discovery of these discrepancies led us to review extensively all corporate addresses generated from the tape files before we computed publication rates.

[15] After we had made these decisions we checked the standard reference on this subject, *Research Centers Directory*, 4th ed., and found that our decision had in each case corresponded to the classification in that volume.

TABLE 6-1   Overall Trends in Departmental Publication Rates, by Field (all major institutions)[a]

	No.	1958	1959	1960	1961	1962	1963	1964	1965	1966	1967	1968	1969	1970	1971	1972
Mathematics	66	9.26	10.94	11.03	11.61	12.89	13.06	13.18	14.24	15.24	15.55	17.77	22.79	24.14	21.44	18.77
Physics	80	19.17	22.45	25.26	25.65	32.41	36.21	40.97	49.59	54.17	58.24	66.77	69.11	72.76	83.52	79.44
Chemistry	88	23.27	24.95	24.63	26.95	25.70	25.10	28.26	35.56	34.50	37.81	43.09	43.67	58.02	49.95	53.57
History	74	2.43	2.68	3.00	3.14	3.70	2.89	3.23	3.31	3.23	3.57	3.04	3.27	3.55	3.28	3.23

[a] Includes all departments rated by Cartter in each field, except those USD institutions not funded in that particular field.

OVERALL TRENDS IN PUBLICATIONS

As a framework for comparing publication trends in funded and in control institutions, it is instructive to look at the general trends within all major universities from 1958 to 1972. Table 6-1 presents the mean departmental publication rates for each field over the period, and Figure 6-1 displays these same data graphically. The total sample consists of all Cartter-rated departments in each field, minus those USD schools that had not received funds in that particular field.

The average rate of publication in leading journals by these departments varied greatly from field to field. Thus, in 1972, the average number of publications per department was 79 in physics, 19 in chemistry, 54 in mathematics, and 3 in history. Publication rates in all three of the science fields, particularly physics, sharply increased over these 15 years, while the rate of publication in history remained about the same. Each of the science fields reached a peak in 1970 or 1971. In chemistry the 1972 rate was greater than the 1971 rate; in mathematics and physics, the 1972 rate was down from the earlier high point.

There are several possible explanations for the slow down in publication rates in science during the latter years. For instance, scientists outside the domain represented by these major universities may be publishing more frequently in the leading journals, thus leaving less space for the scientists from these schools. Or it could be that the relative rates remained the same but somewhat fewer articles were being published in 1971 and 1972 than in 1969 and 1970. Further investigation is needed to reveal the answer to this intriguing question.

COMPARISON OF PUBLICATION RATES IN SCIENCE DEVELOPMENT AND CONTROL INSTITUTIONS

A comparison of publication rates over time in funded and in control institutions reveals changes that show a clear effect of Science Development funds within several science fields but not in the control field of history. These results will be discussed on a field-by-field basis.

Mathematics

Table 6-2 presents the departmental publication rates per year in mathematics for all five groups of institutions. The entries in the body of the table represent the total number of articles published per department in all 20 leading math journals combined. The results are presented separately for all institutions, for public institutions, and for private institutions. In

75

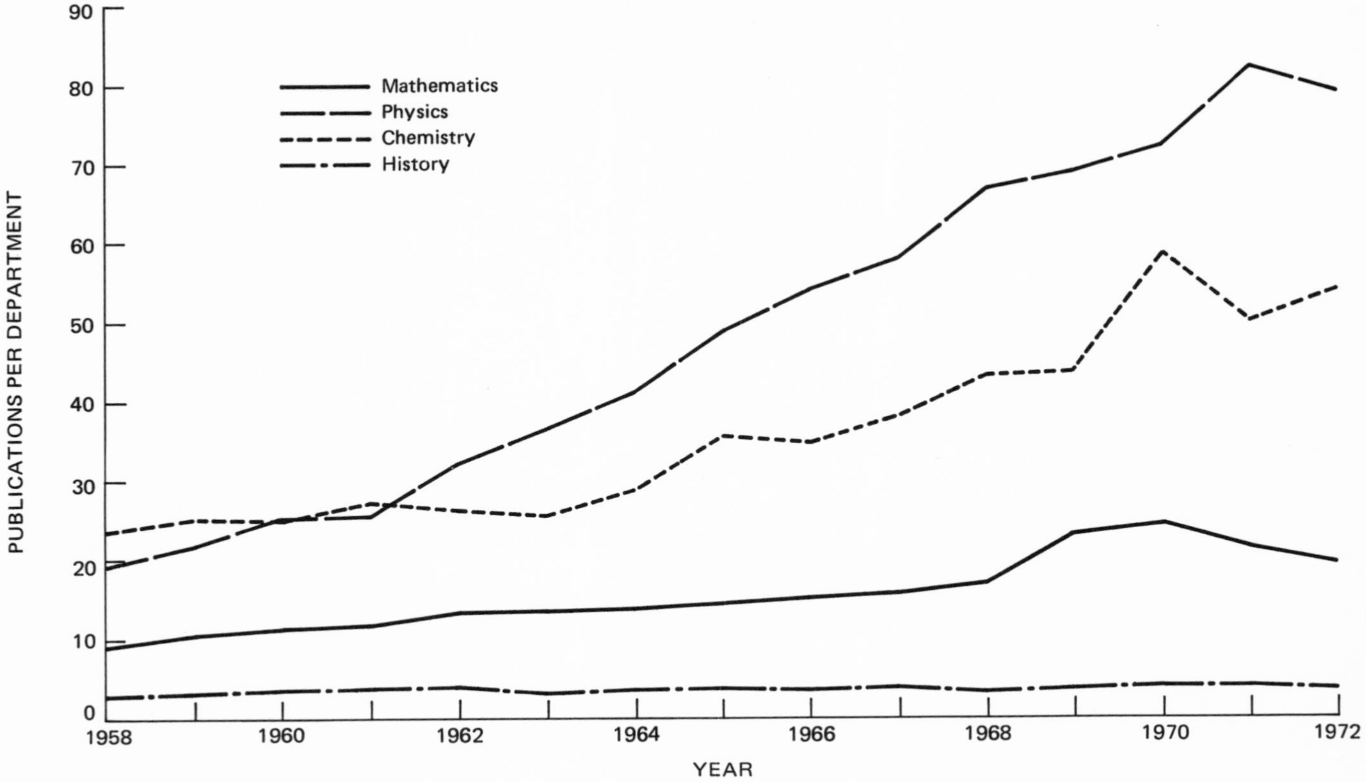

FIGURE 6-1 Overall trends in departmental publication rates, by field (all major institutions).

TABLE 6-2 Departmental Publication Rates in Science Development and Control Institutions: Mathematics

	No.	1958	1959	1960	1961	1962	1963	1964	1965	1966	1967	1968	1969	1970	1971	1972
All Institutions																
USD recipients	15	5.07	8.40	6.47	7.40	8.87	8.07	7.93	8.00	9.87	10.47	15.60	21.40	24.60	23.20	21.73
DSD recipients	5	1.40	1.40	0.40	0.80	1.00	2.40	2.00	1.60	2.60	1.80	3.40	6.60	10.20	10.40	11.20
High controls	17	22.88	27.41	28.00	30.12	33.18	34.59	33.59	37.12	37.41	37.00	38.47	48.82	44.00	40.00	31.88
Medium controls	15	7.73	6.40	8.33	6.53	7.67	7.67	8.87	8.87	9.73	11.00	12.80	12.93	18.60	14.67	13.93
Low controls	16	1.44	1.69	1.81	2.56	2.13	1.63	2.38	3.00	3.94	4.19	4.81	7.94	9.31	7.50	7.00
Public Institutions																
USD recipients	9	4.44	8.44	5.67	7.11	9.67	7.67	8.22	10.00	11.67	12.67	15.44	21.89	27.89	26.89	25.44
DSD recipients	2	3.50	3.00	0.50	1.50	2.00	5.00	3.50	3.50	6.50	3.00	4.50	12.50	22.00	21.00	23.00
High controls	6	25.17	32.00	31.67	39.83	42.17	43.50	43.17	52.67	61.50	57.50	61.50	80.67	72.67	64.67	49.83
Medium controls	8	4.88	4.88	8.00	5.25	5.25	4.75	5.63	7.38	9.00	8.63	12.38	10.00	19.63	14.25	13.38
Low controls	10	1.50	2.40	2.30	3.40	2.70	2.20	3.40	4.10	5.30	6.20	6.20	10.90	12.70	10.50	9.90
Private Institutions																
USD recipients	6	6.00	8.33	7.67	7.83	7.67	8.67	7.50	5.00	7.17	7.17	15.83	20.67	19.67	17.67	16.17
DSD recipients	3	0.0	0.33	0.33	0.33	0.33	0.67	1.00	0.33	0.0	1.00	2.67	2.67	2.33	3.33	3.33
High controls	11	21.64	24.91	26.00	24.82	28.27	29.73	28.36	28.64	24.27	25.82	25.91	31.45	28.36	26.55	22.09
Medium controls	7	11.00	8.14	8.71	8.00	10.43	11.00	12.57	10.57	10.57	13.71	13.29	16.29	17.43	15.14	14.57
Low controls	6	1.33	0.50	1.00	1.17	1.17	0.67	0.67	1.17	1.67	0.83	2.50	3.00	3.67	2.50	2.17

TABLE 6-3 Publication per Faculty Member in Science Development and Control Institutions: Mathematics

	No.	1958	1959	1960	1961	1962	1963	1964	1965	1966	1967	1968	1969	1970	1971	1972
All Institutions																
USD recipients	15	0.25	0.41	0.32	0.30	0.37	0.33	0.33	0.21	0.26	0.28	0.41	0.51	0.58	0.55	0.52
DSD recipients	5	0.10	0.10	0.03	0.06	0.07	0.17	0.14	0.07	0.12	0.08	0.15	0.20	0.31	0.31	0.34
High controls	17	0.91	1.09	1.12	1.02	1.12	1.17	1.14	0.86	0.86	0.85	0.89	1.17	1.05	0.96	0.76
Medium controls	15	0.32	0.26	0.34	0.24	0.28	0.28	0.33	0.24	0.26	0.30	0.34	0.36	0.52	0.41	0.39
Low controls	16	0.10	0.12	0.13	0.14	0.12	0.09	0.13	0.13	0.17	0.18	0.21	0.28	0.32	0.26	0.24
Public Institutions																
USD recipients	9	0.20	0.38	0.26	0.25	0.35	0.27	0.29	0.23	0.26	0.29	0.35	0.43	0.55	0.53	0.50
DSD recipients	2	0.20	0.17	0.03	0.08	0.11	0.28	0.19	0.14	0.26	0.12	0.18	0.29	0.51	0.48	0.53
High controls	6	0.68	0.87	0.86	0.84	0.88	0.91	0.91	0.67	0.79	0.74	0.79	1.09	0.98	0.87	0.67
Medium controls	8	0.17	0.17	0.28	0.16	0.16	0.15	0.18	0.17	0.20	0.19	0.28	0.23	0.45	0.32	0.30
Low controls	10	0.08	0.13	0.12	0.15	0.12	0.10	0.15	0.14	0.18	0.21	0.21	0.29	0.34	0.28	0.26
Private Institutions																
USD recipients	6	0.33	0.46	0.43	0.42	0.41	0.46	0.40	0.18	0.26	0.26	0.57	0.70	0.66	0.60	0.54
DSD recipients	3	0.0	0.03	0.03	0.03	0.03	0.06	0.09	0.02	0.0	0.05	0.13	0.10	0.09	0.13	0.13
High controls	11	1.16	1.34	1.40	1.26	1.43	1.51	1.44	1.17	0.99	1.06	1.06	1.30	1.17	1.09	0.91
Medium controls	7	0.57	0.43	0.46	0.38	0.50	0.52	0.60	0.36	0.36	0.47	0.46	0.62	0.66	0.57	0.55
Low controls	6	0.24	0.09	0.18	0.12	0.12	0.07	0.07	0.09	0.14	0.07	0.20	0.22	0.27	0.18	0.16

addition, Figure 6-2 presents this information more dramatically for USD institutions and medium controls. As the table shows, the publication rates of departments in each group increased over time, except in the case of the high controls, which showed a slight decrease. The most dramatic increase occurred in the USD schools between 1968 and 1970, after the funding. It is conceivable that some of the loss shown by the high controls can be attributed to the transfer of faculty from those schools to the USD and other control schools.

In examining these tables and graphs, one should bear in mind the time lag involved. Although the Science Development program was launched in 1965, many institutions did not receive funds until 1967 or 1968. Before the effects of the funding could be reflected in publication rates, time was needed for new faculty to be hired, for the faculty to produce papers based on their research, and for the journals to review and publish those papers. Presumably, in light of all these factors combined, one would first expect to see the effects of Science Development funding in 1968–1970 (perhaps earlier if a faculty member listed his new institution on articles in press).

A further examination of Table 6-2 reveals that the improved publication rate of the USD and medium control institutions, the widening gap between them, and the drop in the publication rate of the high controls, were more pronounced in the public than in the private sector.

Thus, it is clear that departmental publication rates in mathematics increased much more dramatically in funded than in control institutions. As we saw in Chapter 5, Science Development funds allowed the recipient institutions to expand their faculties considerably. Obviously, the next question is, "Was the increase in publication rates simply a function of the larger staff size, or did the publication rate per person increase as well?" Table 6-3 presents data on the publication rate per faculty member in a format analogous to that in Table 6-2. Bear in mind that, as noted in Chapter 5, data on faculty size were available for only four points in time. Thus, in the analyses reported below, the data have been extrapolated on the following basis:

- 1958 data for 1958, 1959, 1960;
- 1962 data for 1961 through 1964;
- 1966 data for 1965 through 1968;
- 1970 data for 1969 through 1972.

Some minor discontinuities in the graphs (e.g., between 1968 and 1969) may be attributable in part to the shift in the basis for computing faculty size between those two years.

As Table 6-3 indicates the publication rate per faculty member increased

79

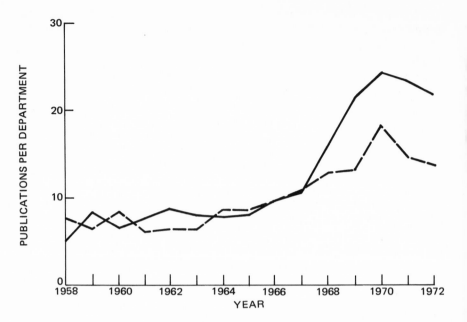

FIGURE 6-2 Departmental publication rates in science development and control institutions: mathematics.

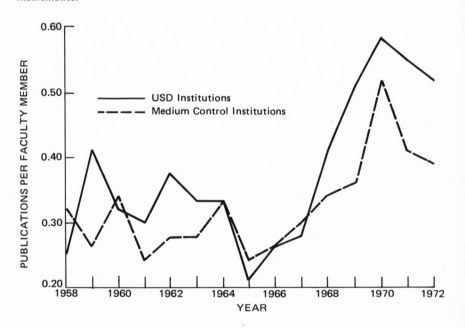

FIGURE 6-3 Publications per faculty member in science development and control institutions: mathematics.

80

much more in funded than in control institutions.[16] (Figure 6-3 presents graphically the trends in per faculty member publication rates for USD and for medium control institutions.) Once again, the changes were much sharper in the public than in the private sector.

Finally, a comparison of the departmental and per person publication trends in institutions with substantial federal science support vs. those with only moderate support revealed that Science Development funding had a more dramatic effect on less affluent institutions.

Physics

Table 6-4 presents the departmental publication rates for the field of physics, including separate breakdowns for public and for private institutions. Figure 6-4 illustrates the trends in the USD and medium control groups. Though in the earlier years USD schools remained about equal to the controls in terms of publication rate, from 1970–1972 they surpassed the controls. The trends for the public and private sectors were about the same.

In a comparison of publication trends in affluent and in less affluent institutions, the funding effect was apparent only in those institutions that received moderate federal science support.

Examination of the data on per person productivity (Table 6-5, Figure 6-5) reveals that the USD scientists consistently trailed below those from the medium controls until 1972, when the positions were reversed. In the private sector the changeover occurred earlier, in 1971. This small effect was seen in the moderately funded schools, but not in those receiving substantial federal science support.

The high controls suffered no setback in physics. In the private sector especially, both the departmental publication rate and the individual publication rate continued to rise.

Chemistry

Table 6-6 presents the publication data for the field of chemistry, including separate breakdowns for public and for private institutions. Figure 6-6 portrays these data for the USD schools and the medium controls.

In comparing all USD and medium controls we find virtually no effect; in only one postfunding year did the former exceed the latter in publications noticeably. There does appear to be a slight effect in the public domain, however.

[16] Note that these rates were computed by dividing the total number of publications per group by the number of faculty members in that group; this straightforward procedure eliminated the distortion that can be caused by differing departmental sizes when one averages rates computed on a per department basis.

81

TABLE 6-4   Departmental Publication Rates in Science Development and Control Institutions: Physics

	No.	1958	1959	1960	1961	1962	1963	1964	1965	1966	1967	1968	1969	1970	1971	1972
All Institutions																
USD recipients	25	13.52	16.16	17.96	18.92	23.80	27.52	29.80	33.20	37.48	43.60	50.96	53.04	63.00	69.48	74.92
DSD recipients	9	3.67	3.22	5.22	4.89	6.89	7.73	9.44	9.78	12.89	12.67	19.22	17.89	21.11	25.89	25.56
High controls	14	63.21	75.36	85.21	83.57	106.00	117.00	137.00	166.71	185.29	182.29	207.21	207.57	212.79	242.71	224.64
Medium controls	18	14.67	15.61	17.06	18.39	23.28	25.17	26.78	37.56	35.61	46.00	49.11	54.61	51.39	60.61	53.28
Low controls	19	1.42	2.11	2.58	2.68	3.95	4.16	5.21	5.74	6.32	7.16	10.42	12.89	15.16	18.89	15.32
Public Institutions																
USD recipients	16	13.13	16.31	16.94	18.06	24.44	28.31	30.25	34.94	39.00	46.44	57.00	58.25	78.25	82.25	89.81
DSD recipients	6	2.67	2.67	3.67	3.83	5.00	5.83	7.00	8.00	11.33	10.17	17.17	16.17	22.00	28.83	26.33
High controls	4	61.00	84.25	92.00	95.75	121.75	121.75	136.00	188.50	184.75	176.25	220.00	201.00	213.00	260.25	250.75
Medium controls	8	15.75	20.13	22.75	21.25	27.75	36.13	33.38	47.38	44.25	53.88	60.88	73.75	64.50	86.75	68.25
Low controls	13	1.77	2.46	3.08	3.23	4.69	4.62	5.46	7.38	8.08	8.77	13.15	15.77	17.77	23.77	20.08
Private Institutions																
USD recipients	9	14.22	15.89	19.78	20.44	22.67	26.11	29.00	30.11	34.78	38.56	40.22	43.78	35.89	46.78	48.44
DSD recipients	3	5.67	4.33	8.33	7.00	10.67	11.67	14.33	13.33	16.00	17.67	23.33	21.33	19.33	20.00	24.00
High controls	10	64.10	71.80	82.50	78.70	99.70	115.10	137.40	158.00	185.50	184.70	202.10	210.20	212.70	235.70	214.20
Medium controls	10	13.80	12.00	12.50	16.10	19.70	16.40	21.50	29.70	28.70	39.70	39.70	39.30	40.90	39.70	41.30
Low controls	6	0.67	1.33	1.50	1.50	2.33	3.17	4.67	2.17	2.50	3.67	4.50	6.67	9.50	8.33	5.00

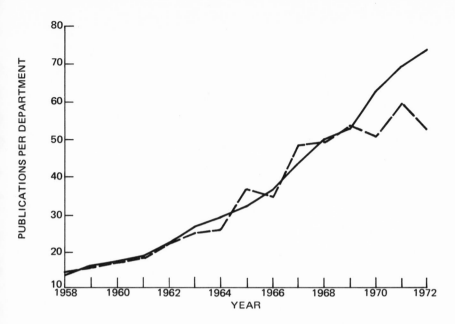

FIGURE 6-4 Departmental publication rates in science development and control institutions: physics.

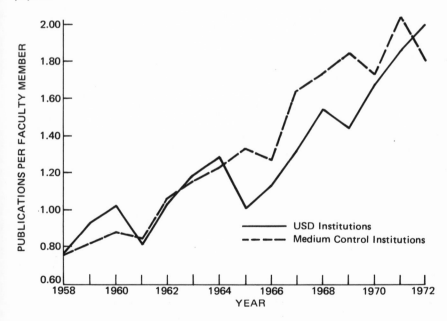

FIGURE 6-5 Publications per faculty member in science development and control institutions: physics.

TABLE 6-5 Publications per Faculty Member in Science Development and Control Institutions: Physics

	No.	1958	1959	1960	1961	1962	1963	1964	1965	1966	1967	1968	1969	1970	1971	1972
All Institutions																
USD recipients	25	0.77	0.92	1.02	0.81	1.02	1.18	1.28	1.00	1.13	1.32	1.54	1.42	1.68	1.86	2.00
DSD recipients	9	0.39	0.35	0.56	0.39	0.54	0.61	0.75	0.55	0.73	0.72	1.09	0.74	0.88	1.07	1.06
High controls	14	2.38	2.84	3.21	2.47	3.14	3.46	4.05	4.29	4.77	4.69	5.33	4.95	5.07	5.79	5.36
Medium controls	18	0.76	0.81	0.88	0.84	1.06	1.15	1.22	1.33	1.26	1.62	1.73	1.84	1.73	2.04	1.80
Low controls	19	0.15	0.22	0.27	0.23	0.34	0.36	0.45	0.36	0.40	0.45	0.66	0.68	0.80	0.99	0.80
Public Institutions																
USD recipients	16	0.72	0.90	0.93	0.74	1.01	1.17	1.25	0.96	1.07	1.28	1.57	1.36	1.83	1.92	2.09
DSD recipients	6	0.29	0.29	0.40	0.32	0.41	0.48	0.58	0.46	0.65	0.58	0.98	0.60	0.81	1.07	0.98
High controls	4	1.95	2.70	2.94	2.55	3.25	3.25	3.63	4.10	4.02	3.83	4.78	3.77	4.00	4.89	4.71
Medium controls	8	0.62	0.80	0.90	0.77	1.00	1.31	1.21	1.38	1.29	1.57	1.77	2.08	1.82	2.45	1.93
Low controls	13	0.16	0.22	0.28	0.24	0.35	0.34	0.40	0.40	0.43	0.47	0.71	0.70	0.79	1.05	0.89
Private Institutions																
USD recipients	9	0.86	0.96	1.19	0.95	1.05	1.21	1.35	1.11	1.28	1.42	1.48	1.58	1.29	1.68	1.74
DSD recipients	3	0.59	0.45	0.86	0.51	0.78	0.85	1.05	0.74	0.89	0.98	1.30	1.16	1.05	1.09	1.31
High controls	10	2.60	2.91	3.34	2.44	3.09	3.56	4.25	4.39	5.15	5.13	5.61	5.62	5.69	6.30	5.73
Medium controls	10	0.94	0.82	0.85	0.93	1.14	0.95	1.24	1.26	1.22	1.69	1.69	1.57	1.63	1.58	1.65
Low controls	6	0.10	0.20	0.22	0.20	0.32	0.43	0.64	0.22	0.26	0.38	0.47	0.59	0.84	0.74	0.44

TABLE 6-6   Departmental Publication Rates in Science Development and Control Institutions: Chemistry

	No.	1958	1959	1960	1961	1962	1963	1964	1965	1966	1967	1968	1969	1970	1971	1972
All Institutions																
USD recipients	22	20.45	23.55	21.14	24.05	25.23	29.55	27.73	34.27	34.68	39.14	43.23	44.55	63.95	50.36	54.86
DSD recipients	12	11.58	11.25	11.58	12.50	12.58	10.58	13.67	17.08	18.25	20.00	20.58	25.50	33.42	31.08	34.75
High controls	15	57.47	58.13	62.73	64.33	61.60	59.27	65.53	90.00	80.67	85.00	101.73	98.60	124.80	105.87	116.93
Medium controls	17	27.41	31.29	27.06	33.35	27.76	23.59	33.35	36.76	37.94	43.65	47.65	46.06	59.12	55.18	53.94
Low controls	24	5.88	5.96	7.25	7.04	7.21	6.63	7.29	8.75	9.42	10.17	12.04	13.71	19.17	18.29	20.08
Public Institutions																
USD recipients	13	16.31	20.38	18.69	21.08	22.85	26.15	26.00	33.23	33.15	39.69	45.31	48.85	64.77	56.23	61.00
DSD recipients	8	13.38	13.63	13.25	12.63	13.38	12.00	14.25	18.13	19.13	22.75	24.13	27.50	41.50	37.88	45.25
High controls	5	73.20	75.40	77.00	81.80	73.40	72.20	66.00	102.60	100.60	99.00	129.00	126.40	146.20	136.80	153.40
Medium controls	13	29.31	33.00	27.77	34.77	28.38	24.23	34.69	36.92	35.85	40.77	47.23	47.00	60.46	57.62	54.69
Low controls	13	5.69	6.00	6.62	6.54	7.15	5.62	7.31	10.31	10.15	10.69	12.38	15.92	21.38	22.62	20.92
Private Institutions																
USD recipients	9	26.44	28.11	24.67	28.33	28.67	34.44	30.22	35.78	36.89	38.33	40.22	38.33	62.78	41.89	46.00
DSD recipients	4	8.00	6.50	8.25	12.25	11.00	7.75	12.50	15.00	16.50	14.50	13.50	21.50	17.25	17.50	13.75
High controls	10	49.60	49.50	55.60	55.60	55.70	52.80	65.30	83.70	70.70	78.00	88.10	84.70	114.10	90.40	98.70
Medium controls	4	21.25	25.75	24.75	28.75	25.75	21.50	29.00	36.25	44.75	53.00	49.00	43.00	54.75	47.25	51.50
Low controls	11	6.09	5.91	8.00	7.64	7.27	7.82	7.27	6.91	8.55	9.55	11.64	11.09	16.55	13.18	19.09

TABLE 6-7   Publications per Faculty Member in Science Development and Control Institutions: Chemistry

	No.	1958	1959	1960	1961	1962	1963	1964	1965	1966	1967	1968	1969	1970	1971	1972
All Institutions																
USD recipients	22	1.13	1.30	1.17	1.18	1.24	1.45	1.36	1.29	1.31	1.48	1.63	1.42	2.05	1.61	1.75
DSD recipients	12	0.72	0.70	0.72	0.77	0.77	0.65	0.84	0.91	0.97	1.07	1.10	1.03	1.35	1.26	1.41
High controls	15	2.62	2.65	2.86	2.57	2.46	2.37	2.62	3.18	2.85	3.01	3.60	3.50	4.43	3.75	4.15
Medium controls	17	1.27	1.45	1.25	1.41	1.17	1.00	1.41	1.37	1.41	1.62	1.77	1.57	2.01	1.88	1.83
Low controls	24	0.49	0.50	0.61	0.52	0.54	0.49	0.54	0.56	0.60	0.65	0.76	0.76	1.06	1.01	1.11
Public Institutions																
USD recipients	13	0.86	1.08	0.99	0.98	1.06	1.21	1.20	1.11	1.11	1.32	1.51	1.37	1.81	1.58	1.71
DSD recipients	8	0.71	0.72	0.70	0.69	0.73	0.66	0.78	0.86	0.91	1.08	1.14	0.95	1.43	1.31	1.56
High controls	5	2.09	2.15	2.20	2.28	2.05	2.02	1.84	2.54	2.49	2.45	3.19	2.71	3.14	2.94	3.29
Medium controls	13	1.25	1.41	1.19	1.38	1.13	0.96	1.38	1.28	1.25	1.42	1.64	1.49	1.92	1.83	1.74
Low controls	13	0.42	0.45	0.49	0.44	0.48	0.38	0.49	0.58	0.57	0.60	0.70	0.74	0.99	1.05	0.97
Private Institutions																
USD recipients	9	1.58	1.68	1.47	1.53	1.54	1.86	1.63	1.67	1.72	1.79	1.88	1.54	2.52	1.68	1.85
DSD recipients	4	0.74	0.60	0.77	1.00	0.90	0.63	1.02	1.07	1.18	1.04	0.96	1.34	1.08	1.09	0.86
High controls	10	3.22	3.21	3.61	2.84	2.84	2.69	3.33	3.77	3.18	3.51	3.97	4.46	6.01	4.76	5.19
Medium controls	4	1.33	1.61	1.55	1.55	1.39	1.16	1.57	1.75	2.16	2.55	2.36	1.89	2.41	2.08	2.26
Low controls	11	0.60	0.59	0.79	0.66	0.63	0.67	0.63	0.52	0.64	0.71	0.87	0.80	1.19	0.95	1.37

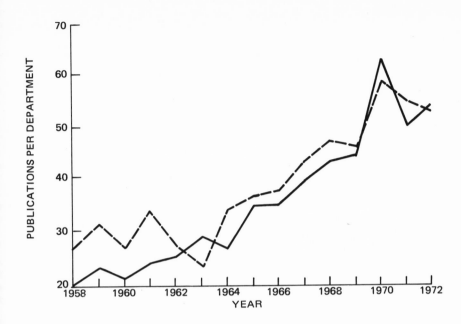

FIGURE 6-6 Departmental publication rates in science development and control institutions: chemistry.

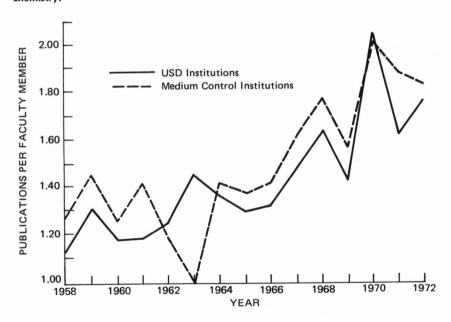

FIGURE 6-7 Publications per faculty member in science development and control institutions: chemistry.

87

TABLE 6-8 Departmental Publication Rates in Science Development and Control Institutions: History

	No.	1958	1959	1960	1961	1962	1963	1964	1965	1966	1967	1968	1969	1970	1971	1972
All Institutions																
USD recipients	24	2.33	2.21	2.88	3.04	3.17	2.33	3.38	2.50	2.92	2.63	2.63	3.04	3.50	2.75	3.38
High controls	14	6.29	6.57	6.71	7.86	9.29	7.21	7.36	9.29	6.71	7.86	6.36	7.43	7.57	7.43	7.07
Medium controls	18	1.72	2.50	2.50	2.28	3.00	2.11	2.17	2.17	2.94	3.22	2.89	2.61	2.72	2.72	2.44
Low controls	18	0.28	0.44	0.78	0.44	0.78	1.06	0.89	0.89	1.22	1.83	1.17	1.00	1.33	1.33	0.83
Public Institutions																
USD recipients	14	2.43	2.29	3.36	3.57	3.21	2.57	3.36	3.36	3.29	2.86	3.36	3.36	4.50	3.36	4.50
High controls	4	6.50	6.75	6.25	7.00	9.25	6.25	7.75	11.00	6.25	9.00	7.25	6.50	9.00	10.50	7.00
Medium controls	10	2.30	3.60	2.80	2.80	3.60	2.50	2.50	2.70	4.00	3.80	3.50	3.00	3.90	4.30	3.40
Low controls	9	0.22	0.67	0.78	0.44	0.56	0.67	1.22	1.00	0.78	2.11	1.22	0.67	1.00	0.78	1.11
Private Institutions																
USD recipients	10	2.20	2.10	2.20	2.30	3.10	2.00	3.40	1.30	2.40	2.30	1.60	2.60	2.10	1.90	1.80
High controls	10	6.20	6.50	6.90	8.20	9.30	7.60	7.20	8.60	6.90	7.40	6.00	7.80	7.00	6.20	7.10
Medium controls	8	1.00	1.13	2.13	1.63	2.25	1.63	1.75	1.50	1.63	2.50	2.13	2.13	1.25	0.75	1.25
Low controls	9	0.33	0.22	0.78	0.44	1.00	1.44	0.56	0.78	1.67	1.56	1.11	1.33	1.67	1.89	0.56

There is no effect on per person publication in chemistry (except among those schools characterized by moderate amounts of total federal support for science where some impact of Science Development funding is evident) (Table 6-7, Figure 6-7).

One might hypothesize that the difference between these findings and those for mathematics and physics reflect a greater lag time involved in chemistry publication.

History

As Figure 6-1 indicates, during the entire period from 1958 to 1972, the publication rate in history, the control field, was far below that in the three science fields. Moreover, there was no pattern of growth (Table 6-8, Figure 6-8); indeed, in the 74 history departments considered, the per faculty publication rate declined (Table 6-9, Figure 6-9). Though funded institutions may have improved their standing slightly relative to control institutions, that trend is by no means clear.

A Multivariate Analysis of Impact

The results so far discussed are essentially zero-order effects, providing a descriptive profile of trends in publication rates in the experimental and control institutions. They do not take into account other factors (e.g., departmental graduate enrollments) that may influence these differences. The next step was to examine the changes in these trends when such related factors are controlled through use of a linear prediction model.[17]

The method used for this multivariate analysis was similar to that used in the study of changes in faculty size. A number of dimensions from a time period clearly prior to the initiation of the Science Development program (1959–1961) were selected to represent those factors that were most likely to be related to subsequent rates of publication. This became the independent variable set for a series of multiple regression equations:

1. Total (departmental) graduate enrollment;
2. Departmental faculty size;
3. Departmental doctorate production;
4. Total federal science support for the institution.

As before, the variables were created by taking the average of the values for the years 1959–1961, where possible. In the case of faculty size only

[17] Even though we collected 15 years' worth of longitudinal data, there were still not sufficient trend data to use some of the statistical techniques developed by Box and Taio, and others, as a means of assessing the discontinuity in the curves.

TABLE 6-9 Publications per Faculty Member in Science Development and Control Institutions: History

	No.	1958	1959	1960	1961	1962	1963	1964	1965	1966	1967	1968	1969	1970	1971	1972
All Institutions																
USD recipients	24	0.15	0.14	0.18	0.17	0.17	0.13	0.18	0.10	0.12	0.11	0.11	0.11	0.13	0.10	0.12
High controls	14	0.26	0.27	0.28	0.28	0.33	0.26	0.26	0.26	0.19	0.22	0.18	0.24	0.24	0.24	0.23
Medium controls	18	0.12	0.17	0.17	0.13	0.17	0.12	0.12	0.09	0.13	0.14	0.13	0.10	0.10	0.10	0.09
Low controls	18	0.03	0.05	0.08	0.04	0.06	0.09	0.07	0.05	0.07	0.11	0.07	0.05	0.07	0.07	0.04
Public Institutions																
USD recipients	14	0.15	0.14	0.21	0.18	0.16	0.13	0.17	0.12	0.12	0.10	0.12	0.10	0.14	0.10	0.14
High controls	4	0.24	0.25	0.23	0.23	0.30	0.20	0.25	0.22	0.13	0.18	0.15	0.12	0.17	0.19	0.13
Medium controls	10	0.13	0.20	0.16	0.13	0.17	0.12	0.12	0.09	0.14	0.13	0.12	0.09	0.12	0.13	0.10
Low controls	9	0.03	0.08	0.09	0.04	0.06	0.07	0.12	0.06	0.05	0.13	0.07	0.03	0.05	0.04	0.05
Private Institutions																
USD recipients	10	0.15	0.14	0.15	0.14	0.18	0.12	0.20	0.06	0.12	0.11	0.08	0.12	0.10	0.09	0.08
High controls	10	0.27	0.28	0.30	0.31	0.35	0.29	0.27	0.29	0.23	0.25	0.20	0.35	0.32	0.28	0.32
Medium controls	8	0.10	0.11	0.21	0.13	0.17	0.13	0.14	0.10	0.11	0.17	0.14	0.12	0.07	0.04	0.07
Low controls	9	0.03	0.02	0.07	0.03	0.07	0.10	0.04	0.05	0.10	0.09	0.07	0.07	0.09	0.10	0.03

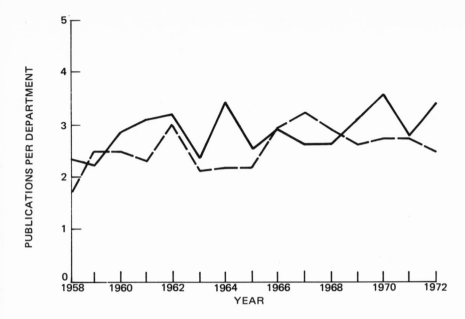

FIGURE 6-8 Departmental publication rates in science development and control institutions: history.

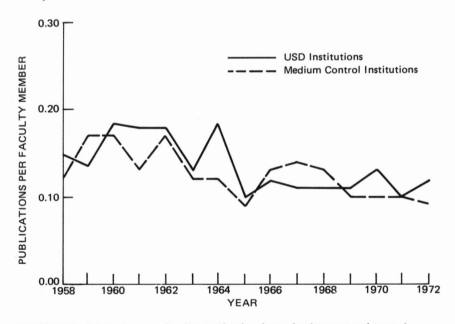

FIGURE 6-9 Publications per faculty member in science development and control institutions: history.

91

those numbers for 1958 and 1962 were averaged. For federal support for science, data for the year 1963 (the earliest available) were used.

The independent variables taken together represent the status of a given department with respect to key related dimensions prior to funding. These variables were systematically regressed on publication rate for each year from 1965 through 1972. Table 6-10 presents the results from these regressions and includes not only the multiple correlations but also the regression coefficients for each independent variable in each equation.

Several mechanisms were used to test for and isolate the grant effects. First, a dummy variable indicating whether or not a department received a grant was created. Then the partial correlation between this variable and publication rate (the criterion) was computed while all of the predictor variables were controlled. The size of this partial in a given year reflects the variation in publication rate for that year that can be attributed uniquely to the receipt of the Science Development grant. Each of these partials is presented in Table 6-10.

Data collected by the National Science Foundation yielded information about the total amount of federal support received by each department in 1968. The partial correlations of this variable with publication rate are also included in Table 6-10.[18] The differences between these measures and the grant partials provide a rough indication of the special impact of Science Development funds.

As a further mechanism for examining the effects of Science Development the equations developed in this analysis were used to generate predicted publication rates for each department for each year. These "expected" figures were then subtracted from *actual* publication rates, yielding a residual score for each school for each year. Finally, these residual scores were averaged over the experimental and control groups (Figure 6-10).

In other words, this linear model allowed us to predict publication rates in each school for each year on the basis of all key factors but Science Development funding. Differences in the predictive efficacy of the model between the experimental and the control groups (as measured by the gap between these predicted rates and the actual number of publications produced) indicate that the funding had an impact on publication rates.

Examination of the results of these analyses reveals an impact of Science Development funds on publications in each of the science fields but not in history, the control field. In all three science fields the USD and medium

---

[18] Partial correlations from these analyses of about 0.20 or more are statistically significant. In particular, the threshhold values for each field are mathematics, 0.21; physics, 0.18; chemistry, 0.18; and history, 0.20.

control residuals spread significantly as time passes: The USD productivity exceeds predictions, while the control productivity falls below the predicted levels.

The reader should note that the residual scores provide a much better indication of impact than do the partial correlations. The former scores have been aggregated for each of the five groups; thus, it is possible to compare the USD trends with those of the medium controls, the most meaningful control group. In contrast, construction of the dummy variable used in the partials required putting all controls (high, medium, and low) into one "nonfunded" category. As a result, direct comparison of funded departments with the medium controls is not possible with the partial correlations.

As Table 6-10 and Figure 6-10 show, the unique impact of Science Development was manifested most dramatically in mathematics. Note that the partial correlations between Science Development funding and publications for 1970, 1971, and 1972 were very high (for 1972, the figure was 0.33). Note also that the effect of these funds, as reflected in the partials, greatly exceeds that of all federal funds to the department. That is, Science Development grants in particular had a marked effect on publication by faculty in key mathematics journals.

In chemistry the unique impact of Science Development funding was reflected in small positive partials that do not approach significance. The largest impact occurred in 1970.

In physics, the partials were neither significant nor positive. In both chemistry and physics, the partials for all federal funds were much higher than those for Science Development funds alone.

Table 6-11 and Figure 6-11 present comparable data from a multivariate analysis of the effects of funding on per person productivity. Residuals were calculated for each of the three years for which faulty size data were available. The only field in which these results indicate a possible Science Development impact is chemistry, where by 1970 the USD recipients were performing much better than the medium controls.

Summary

Taken together, the zero-order and multivariate results for total faculty productivity and per person productivity paint the following picture. Science Development funding had an impact on departmental productivity in each of the three science fields. In chemistry this effect was revealed only through the multivariate analyses, but in math and physics it was clear from inspection of the zero-order trends. The improvement in departmen-

TABLE 6-10 Prediction of Publication Rates, 1965–1972

	1965	1966	1967	1968	1969	1970	1971	1972
Mathematics (N = 65)								
Multiple correlation	0.89	0.88	0.84	0.86	0.81	0.74	0.77	0.69
Regression coefficients[a]								
Faculty size	0.03	0.03	0.03	0.07	0.09	0.15	0.13	0.19
Doctorate production	0.37	0.35	0.41	0.28	0.33	0.25	0.16	0.19
Enrollment	0.79	0.97	0.85	0.80	0.82	0.91	0.78	0.87
Science funding to university	-0.25	-0.44	-0.42	-0.23	-0.38	-0.52	-0.25	-0.52
Partial correlations[b]								
Science development grant	-0.05	0.01	-0.02	0.16	0.20	0.21	0.31	0.33
All federal funds to department	0.02	-0.02	-0.07	0.18	0.24	0.18	0.12	0.18
Chemistry (N = 88)								
Multiple correlation	0.88	0.87	0.86	0.84	0.86	0.83	0.84	0.82
Regression coefficients[a]								
Faculty size	0.03	-0.01	0.10	0.05	0.07	0.13	0.18	0.17
Doctorate production	0.57	0.50	0.51	0.42	0.59	0.37	0.46	0.51
Enrollment	0.16	0.39	0.16	0.37	0.18	0.31	0.13	0.10
Science funding to university	0.18	0.02	0.16	0.03	0.06	0.10	0.15	0.13
Partial correlations[b]								
Science development grant	0.03	0.05	0.07	-0.03	0.08	0.12	0.05	0.09
All federal funds to department	0.48	0.50	0.48	0.35	0.44	0.63	0.34	0.32

Physics (N = 82)

Multiple correlation	0.92	0.92	0.91	0.91	0.88	0.85	0.87	0.88
Regression coefficients[a]								
Faculty size	0.12	0.16	0.18	0.16	0.22	0.29	0.24	0.20
Doctorate production	0.69	0.67	0.64	0.63	0.56	0.41	0.47	0.58
Enrollment	0.04	−0.02	−0.03	−0.00	−0.09	−0.01	−0.01	0.04
Science funding to university	0.15	0.18	0.20	0.19	0.27	0.27	0.26	0.15
Partial correlations[b]								
Science development grant	−0.17	−0.12	−0.09	−0.07	−0.05	0.02	−0.01	0.11
All federal funds to department	0.06	0.37	0.36	0.35	0.28	0.23	0.19	0.16

History (N = 72)

Multiple correlation	0.86	0.70	0.78	0.80	0.68	0.72	0.76	0.72
Regression coefficients[a]								
Faculty size	0.19	0.12	0.06	0.08	−0.13	0.38	0.05	0.29
Doctorate production	0.39	0.27	0.57	0.58	0.43	0.19	0.20	0.28
Enrollment	−0.22	−0.64	−0.18	−0.65	−0.19	−0.17	0.55	0.11
Science funding to university	0.59	0.98	0.39	0.84	0.59	0.39	−0.01	0.13
Partial correlations[b]								
Science development grant	−0.07	0.05	−0.11	0.12	0.10	0.11	−0.14	0.17

[a] Regression coefficients are standardized.
[b] Partials controlled for the four variables above.

95

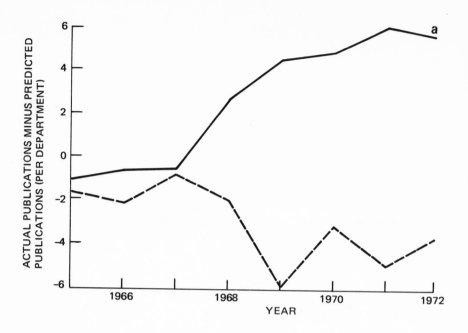

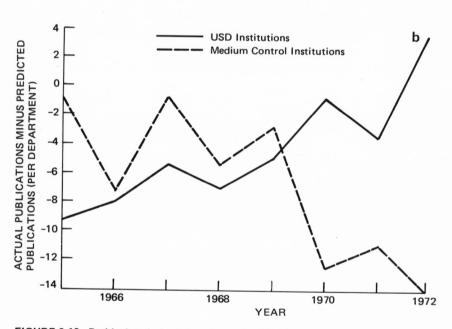

FIGURE 6-10   Residual analysis of departmental publication rates: (a) mathematics, (b) physics, (c) chemistry, (d) history.

96

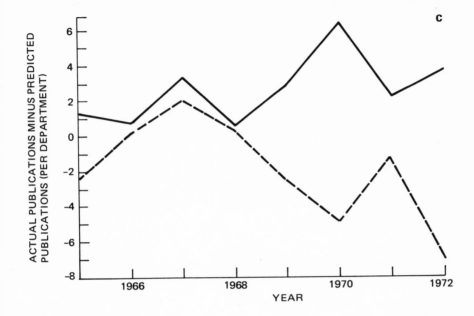

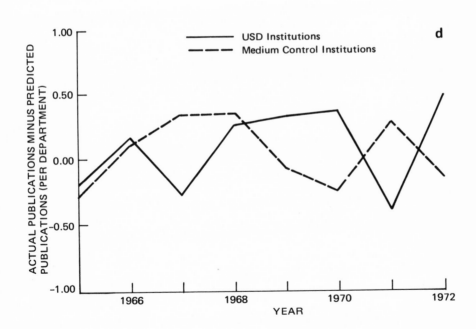

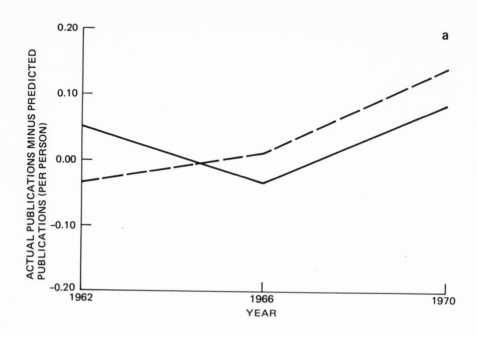

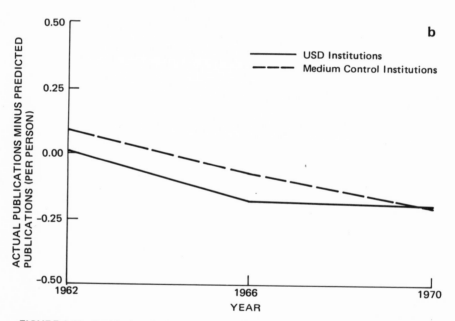

FIGURE 6-11   Residual analysis of publication rates per faculty member: (a) mathematics, (b) physics, (c) chemistry, (d) history.

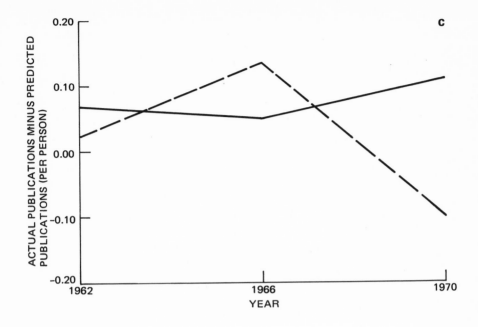

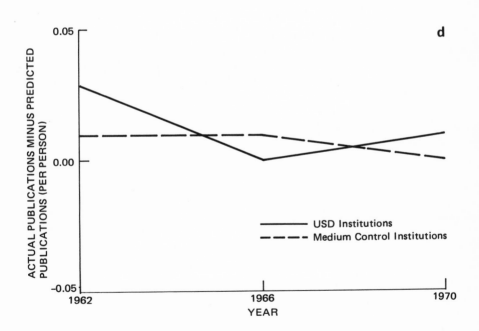

99

TABLE 6-11   Prediction of Publications per Faculty Member

	1962	1966	1970
Mathematics (*N* = 65)			
Multiple correlation	0.61	0.68	0.40
Regression coefficients[a]			
Doctorate production	0.10	0.32	0.01
Enrollment	0.06	0.14	0.20
Science funding to university	0.48	0.30	0.22
Partial correlations[b]			
Science development grant	−0.01	−0.10	0.04
All federal funds to department	0.14	−0.16	0.04
Chemistry (*N* = 87)			
Multiple correlation	0.61	0.62	0.64
Regression coefficients[a]			
Doctorate production	0.16	0.03	0.09
Enrollment	0.28	0.33	0.18
Science funding to university	0.24	0.35	0.44
Partial correlations[b]			
Science development grant	0.04	0.04	0.02
All federal funds to department	0.32	0.42	0.35
Physics (*N* = 82)			
Multiple correlation	0.75	0.83	0.55
Regression coefficients[a]			
Doctorate production	0.63	0.75	0.40
Enrollment	−0.15	−0.14	−0.24
Science funding to university	0.27	0.22	0.35
Partial correlations[b]			
Science development grant	0.00	−0.05	0.09
All federal funds to department	0.16	0.23	0.19
History (*N* = 71)			
Multiple correlation	0.52	0.36	0.41
Regression coefficients[a]			
Doctorate production	0.30	0.23	0.32
Enrollment	−0.27	−0.36	−0.16
Science funding to university	0.45	0.35	0.25
Partial correlations[b]			
Science development grant	0.16	−0.02	0.11

[a] Regression coefficients are standardized.
[b] Partials controlled for the three variables above.

tal publication records at funded institutions was strongest in mathematics, definite in physics, and weakest in chemistry. The trend in mathematics was evident in both the public and private sectors.

There was less impact on per person productivity. The math data seemed to indicate an effect, but the residual analyses raised a question as to whether this effect was a function of Science Development funding or an artifact attributable to other factors. There seemed to be no effect in physics; the multivariate analyses revealed a possible impact in chemistry. No effects were seen in the control field of history.

In short, recipient science departments clearly improved their publication rates with the aid of Science Development funding. But the change was a departmental one, probably the result of the simple increase in faculty size; the effects on per person productivity were minimal.

7 Impact on Graduate Students

Many would argue that the graduate students themselves are the essence of graduate education. Certainly, the future of scientific research lies with those who are currently undergoing this apprenticeship. We turn now to an assessment of the effects of Science Development on graduate enrollments and input characteristics; a study of the output—Ph.D. production—follows in the next chapter. Once again, the goal has been to combine a quantitative measure—enrollments—with an assessment of the impact of funding on quality, defined in terms of the test scores and baccalaureate origins of entering graduate students.

EFFECTS ON GRADUATE ENROLLMENTS

To assess the impact of Science Development funds on graduate enroll- ments, we required a data source providing annual enrollment information that was comparable from field to field and from institution to institution. The source that came closest to meeting these criteria was *Students Enrolled for Advanced Degrees–Institutional Data,* an annual publication of the National Center for Educational Statistics (NCES). Since the NCES did not begin collecting these data until 1959 and since the data for 1971 and 1972 had not been published at the time of the study, our discussion of trends covers only this period (1959–1970), rather than the full 15 years.

From these volumes were extracted two key indicators of enrollment trends at all schools under study for the funded fields of physics, chemistry, and mathematics and for the control field of history: (1) the total graduate enrollment (men and women, full time and part time) and (2) first-year, full-time enrollment (men and women). Both indicators were used because we felt that while it is imperative to examine trends in total enrollments, first-year trends were more likely to be sensitive to the impact of funding.

Part-time students were included in the former measure but excluded in the latter on the grounds that legitimate doctoral aspirants often enroll on a part-time basis while completing their dissertations; conversely, very few serious graduate students begin their studies on a part-time basis.

Overall Enrollment Trends

In Figure 7-1 trends in total enrollments for each of the four fields are plotted; Figure 7-2 depicts trends in first-year, full-time enrollments. These two curves reveal a good deal about the changing graduate student population between 1959 and 1970. Graduate student enrollments in history tended to be larger than those in any of the three sciences. In each field, total graduate enrollments grew more or less steadily, peaking in 1967 and 1968 and then declining; similarly, first-year, full-time enrollments in the sciences grew steadily until the mid-1960s, when they peaked.

Against this background, it is interesting to compare the behavior of Science Development and of control departments.

Trends in Science Development and Control Institutions

Table 7-1 presents average departmental enrollments in mathematics for each year from 1959 to 1970 in each of five groups of institutions: USD recipients, DSD and SSD recipients, high control, medium control, and low control. Data are presented for all institutions, public institutions only, and private institutions only. Figure 7-3 plots the total enrollments for the USD schools and the medium controls; While the "all institutions" data reveal no impact of funding, separate analyses show a difference between the public and private sectors. In the private domain the medium controls exceeded the USDs before, during, and after the grant. However in the public sector, there appears to have been an impact of Science Development funding upon these total graduate enrollments.

Table 7-2 presents data on average first-year, full-time departmental enrollments in mathematics for the same five groups of institutions. In Figure 7-4 the data for the USD recipients and the medium control group have been plotted. There is no impact of the funding on first-year enrollments revealed in these data.

103

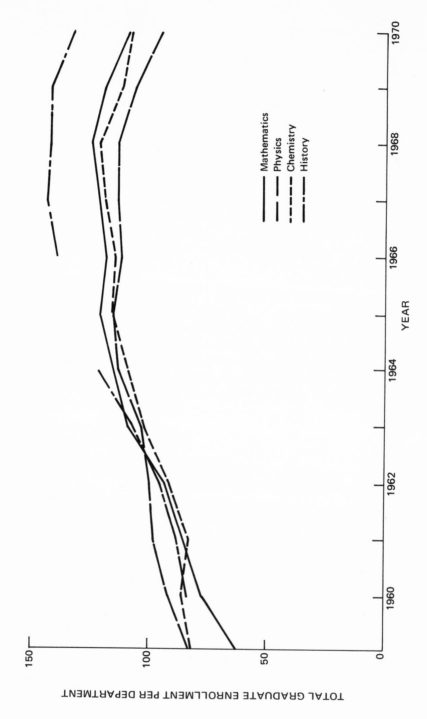

FIGURE 7-1 Overall trends in total graduate enrollments by field (all major institutions).

104

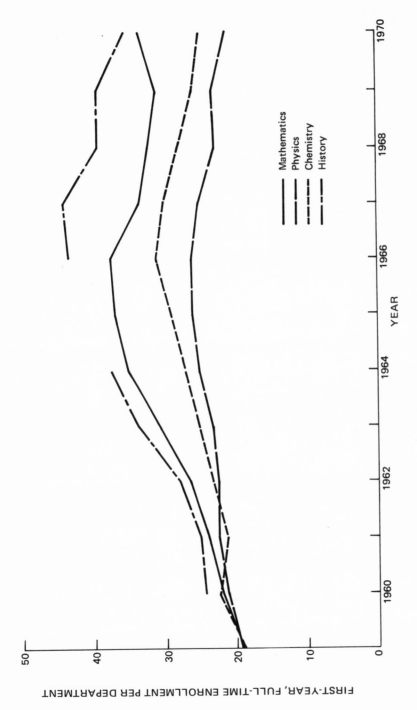

FIGURE 7-2 Overall trends in first-year, full-time graduate enrollments by field (all major institutions).

FIRST-YEAR, FULL-TIME ENROLLMENT PER DEPARTMENT

Mathematics
Physics
Chemistry
History

105

TABLE 7-1 Departmental Enrollments in Science Development and Control Institutions: Mathematics (all graduate students)

	No.	1959	1960	1961	1962	1963	1964	1965	1966	1967	1968	1969	1970
All Institutions													
USD recipients	15	51.87	62.73	77.80	84.27	100.73	105.80	124.07	124.87	133.20	128.67	126.53	117.13
DSD recipients	5	31.80	27.40	30.80	36.80	40.80	52.00	56.40	63.00	58.60	64.80	68.80	61.60
High controls	17	101.76	122.59	134.35	148.65	161.41	164.88	154.65	163.94	165.24	160.88	153.82	148.24
Medium controls	15	60.53	79.20	81.13	86.93	110.87	120.80	124.67	119.47	121.73	144.60	139.20	104.47
Low controls	16	40.44	47.94	52.50	58.50	69.50	74.63	83.38	68.25	68.06	75.56	65.06	71.69
Public Institutions													
USD recipients	9	57.56	72.00	91.67	95.22	115.00	121.00	145.44	145.78	162.00	159.56	161.56	152.78
DSD recipients	2	50.50	38.50	37.50	52.00	53.50	64.00	76.50	84.50	87.00	91.50	91.00	97.00
High controls	6	180.50	214.83	233.50	264.00	292.50	293.00	291.33	319.50	314.00	291.50	278.67	266.67
Medium controls	8	65.13	79.88	81.25	91.50	122.13	137.88	138.75	146.25	137.75	143.75	130.25	123.63
Low controls	10	37.10	45.10	50.40	63.80	76.30	82.60	96.30	76.70	74.40	83.90	70.10	80.00
Private Institutions													
USD recipients	6	43.33	48.83	57.00	67.83	79.33	83.00	92.00	93.50	90.00	82.33	74.00	63.67
DSD recipients	3	19.33	20.00	26.33	26.67	32.33	44.00	43.00	48.67	39.67	47.00	54.00	38.00
High controls	11	58.82	72.27	80.27	85.73	89.91	95.00	80.09	79.09	84.09	89.64	85.73	83.64
Medium controls	7	55.29	78.43	81.00	81.71	98.00	101.29	108.57	88.86	103.43	145.57	149.43	82.57
Low controls	6	46.00	52.67	56.00	49.67	58.17	61.33	61.83	54.17	57.50	61.67	56.67	57.83

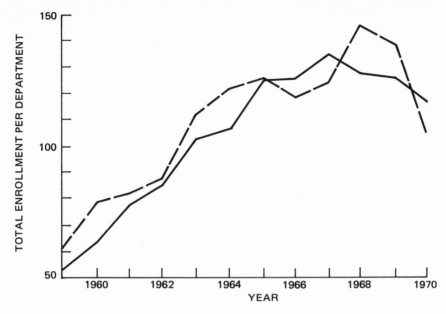

FIGURE 7-3 Departmental enrollments in science development and control institutions (all graduate students): mathematics.

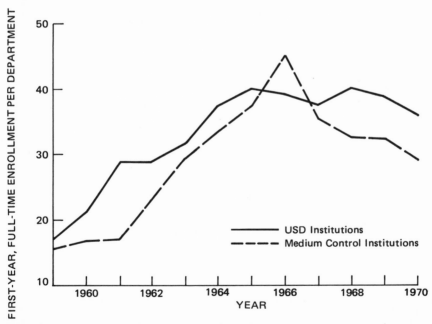

FIGURE 7-4 Departmental enrollments in science development and control institutions (first-year, full-time graduate students only): mathematics.

107

TABLE 7-2 Departmental Enrollments in Science Development and Control Institutions: Mathematics (first-year, full-time graduate students only)

	No.	1959	1960	1961	1962	1963	1964	1965	1966	1967	1968	1969	1970
All Institutions													
USD recipients	15	16.87	21.00	28.53	28.47	31.80	37.07	40.00	38.93	37.40	40.07	38.53	35.87
DSD recipients	5	7.40	8.40	8.20	8.80	11.40	18.20	18.00	16.40	13.00	9.00	15.20	17.00
High controls	17	32.24	40.06	42.06	45.00	46.82	51.94	51.88	50.71	47.18	48.94	47.47	49.82
Medium controls	15	15.40	16.73	16.87	23.07	29.20	33.60	37.00	44.87	35.40	32.27	32.13	28.80
Low controls	16	11.25	10.81	11.81	11.44	15.81	17.13	19.50	18.25	14.75	12.44	11.94	19.44
Public Institutions													
USD recipients	9	16.22	24.33	30.44	33.56	41.22	48.67	53.67	52.89	49.89	56.11	52.89	49.22
DSD recipients	2	12.50	13.00	9.50	13.00	19.00	24.00	25.00	23.50	17.50	7.50	14.50	19.50
High controls	6	60.50	74.00	76.33	80.17	83.17	92.17	93.00	91.00	83.67	91.83	87.83	99.50
Medium controls	8	23.25	22.13	22.13	24.38	34.00	44.75	51.13	59.88	41.88	42.25	37.63	38.13
Low controls	10	13.40	13.60	15.70	14.90	19.90	21.20	24.50	22.40	15.10	13.10	14.80	24.90
Private Institutions													
USD recipients	6	17.83	16.00	25.67	20.83	17.67	19.67	19.50	18.00	18.67	16.00	17.00	15.83
DSD recipients	3	4.00	5.33	7.33	6.00	6.33	14.33	13.33	11.67	10.00	10.00	15.67	15.33
High controls	11	16.82	21.55	23.36	25.82	27.00	30.00	27.20	28.73	27.27	25.55	25.45	22.73
Medium controls	7	6.43	10.57	10.86	21.57	23.71	20.86	20.86	27.71	28.00	20.86	25.86	18.14
Low controls	6	7.67	6.17	5.33	5.67	9.00	10.33	11.17	11.33	14.17	11.33	7.17	10.33

A comparison of total and first-year math enrollments in schools receiving substantial federal science support, as contrasted with those receiving moderate amounts of support, revealed an impact in the former sector. That is, among those schools that received considerable amounts of money for the sciences from all federal sources, the math enrollments at Science Development institutions grew more rapidly than those at control schools. This may indicate that Science Development funds alone are not sufficient to motivate a school to expand enrollments but rather had to be part of a larger picture of relative affluence.

Table 7-3 (total enrollments) and 7-4 (first-year enrollments) and Figure 7-5 (total) and 7-6 (first year) present comparable data for physics. No effect of Science Development funding upon physics enrollments is seen in these tables. However, when substantially funded institutions are compared with moderately funded institutions an effect of Science Development funding on both total enrollments and first-year enrollment is seen in the wealthier schools.

Table 7-5 and 7-6 and Figures 7-7 and 7-8 present the graduate enrollment data for chemistry. Once again, there appears to be no impact of funding on either total or first-year enrollments with the possible exception of the public sector. Here, the USD recipients began with total enrollments quite a bit below those of the medium control groups; by the end of the funding period, however, the two enrollments were about equal.

Finally, Tables 7-7 and 7-8 and Figures 7-9 and 7-10 present graduate enrollment data for the control field of history. No relationship between Science Development funding and either enrollment index is seen in history. First-year enrollments at the USD recipient institutions exceeded those at the medium controls throughout the entire time period.

A Multivariate Analysis of Impact

The same multivariate tests of impact that were employed earlier with respect to faculty size and publication rates were applied to the data on enrollments. That is, a linear model, based on measures reflecting conditions at the institutions well before funding began, was used to estimate total (Table 7-9) and first-year (Table 7-10) graduate enrollments at Science Development institutions and at control institutions for each year between 1965 and 1972. The predictor variables, and the years to which they applied, were publication rate, 1959–1961; faculty size, 1958, 1962; Ph.D. production, 1959–1961; and total federal science funding, 1963.

As before, a series of regression equations predicting enrollments for each year were generated. The total enrollment results are presented in Table 7-9, which includes each multiple correlation coefficient and several partial correlation coefficients: One partial correlation is between enroll-

109

TABLE 7-3 Departmental Enrollments in Science Development and Control Institutions: Physics (all graduate students)

	No.	1959	1960	1961	1962	1963	1964	1965	1966	1967	1968	1969	1970
All Institutions													
USD recipients	25	89.24	99.28	107.80	103.76	112.60	119.68	121.64	118.12	125.80	127.72	116.64	105.60
DSD recipients	9	37.00	50.00	50.11	52.56	58.56	65.56	71.22	77.25	73.33	73.33	68.44	66.13
High controls	14	159.64	165.36	174.79	182.14	183.79	200.29	206.57	200.62	202.50	198.64	196.07	165.07
Medium controls	18	71.00	79.11	82.00	94.11	101.56	101.28	107.72	101.27	107.72	102.22	94.06	83.78
Low controls	19	37.56	44.67	46.88	47.26	46.11	55.37	56.37	50.11	51.94	53.74	49.05	48.63
Public Institutions													
USD recipients	16	84.69	95.94	109.38	105.50	112.38	124.00	128.56	126.75	133.31	140.19	129.56	122.13
DSD recipients	6	33.17	41.17	43.50	49.33	54.17	64.83	69.83	81.40	74.83	73.50	68.50	64.17
High controls	4	213.00	222.50	250.00	253.50	262.00	274.25	281.25	262.75	267.00	264.25	251.25	160.00
Medium controls	8	72.75	82.75	90.13	104.75	111.75	107.50	122.75	122.71	120.63	118.50	109.63	102.50
Low controls	13	44.08	50.92	54.83	56.23	54.15	65.69	66.31	53.75	62.92	65.08	57.85	57.77
Private Institutions													
USD recipients	9	97.33	105.22	105.00	100.67	113.00	112.00	109.33	102.78	112.44	105.56	93.67	76.22
DSD recipients	3	44.67	76.50	63.33	59.00	67.33	67.00	74.00	70.33	70.33	73.00	68.33	72.00
High controls	10	138.30	142.50	144.70	153.60	152.50	170.70	176.70	173.00	176.70	172.40	174.00	167.10
Medium controls	10	69.60	76.20	75.50	85.60	93.40	96.30	95.70	93.75	86.60	89.20	81.60	68.80
Low controls	6	24.50	32.17	27.80	27.83	28.67	33.00	34.83	42.83	30.00	29.17	30.00	28.83

TABLE 7-4 Departmental Enrollments in Science Development and Control Institutions: Physics (first-year, full-time graduate students only)

	No.	1959	1960	1961	1962	1963	1964	1965	1966	1967	1968	1969	1970
All Institutions													
USD recipients	25	18.72	21.84	24.33	23.24	25.88	34.28	30.16	29.64	31.00	26.28	27.56	26.20
DSD recipients	9	9.63	12.71	13.38	10.11	11.67	16.56	13.56	19.13	11.33	9.44	10.22	13.63
High controls	14	38.71	41.29	44.64	42.79	47.43	52.36	47.57	46.15	49.21	41.29	42.07	31.86
Medium controls	18	14.56	15.06	15.28	19.83	18.28	18.56	23.83	21.20	18.50	20.44	18.94	19.35
Low controls	19	8.65	9.81	10.75	11.56	11.44	10.28	12.74	13.47	9.72	10.00	10.83	12.56
Public Institutions													
USD recipients	16	18.69	22.75	27.47	24.94	31.13	42.94	35.56	36.69	38.88	33.63	35.44	34.19
DSD recipients	6	11.33	14.20	14.33	10.67	13.17	19.50	15.83	22.40	11.33	11.17	10.00	15.50
High controls	4	72.00	65.00	64.25	63.25	63.50	65.00	68.25	55.00	61.75	68.75	62.50	43.00
Medium controls	8	19.29	19.88	20.13	27.25	22.38	24.38	35.50	25.00	21.50	25.38	25.50	27.38
Low controls	13	9.08	10.00	11.42	13.77	13.58	11.31	14.85	14.42	12.17	11.46	13.08	14.38
Private Institutions													
USD recipients	9	18.78	20.22	19.11	20.22	16.56	18.89	20.56	17.11	17.00	13.22	13.56	12.00
DSD recipients	3	4.50	9.00	10.50	9.00	8.67	10.67	9.00	13.67	11.33	6.00	10.67	8.00
High controls	10	25.40	31.80	36.80	34.60	41.00	47.30	39.30	42.22	44.20	30.30	33.90	27.40
Medium controls	10	10.89	10.78	11.40	13.90	15.00	13.90	14.50	17.88	16.10	16.50	13.70	12.22
Low controls	6	7.60	9.25	8.75	5.80	7.17	7.60	8.17	11.20	4.83	6.20	5.00	7.80

111

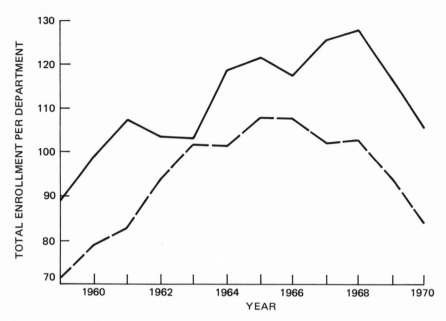

FIGURE 7-5 Departmental enrollments in science development and control institutions (all graduate students): physics.

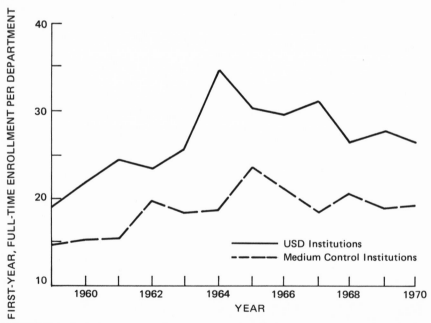

FIGURE 7-6 Departmental enrollments in science development and control institutions (first-year, full-time graduate students only): physics.

112

TABLE 7-5 Departmental Enrollments in Science Development and Control Institutions: Chemistry (all graduate students)

	No.	1959	1960	1961	1962	1963	1964	1965	1966	1967	1968	1969	1970
All Institutions													
USD recipients	22	97.18	101.18	95.09	98.55	111.59	118.23	124.23	126.68	128.82	127.50	120.45	112.14
DSD recipients	12	43.25	46.42	50.17	55.58	58.92	65.92	82.55	82.67	78.92	88.75	83.17	83.83
High controls	15	138.00	143.00	147.13	151.67	168.27	172.47	179.07	184.21	191.60	196.93	179.20	179.20
Medium controls	17	93.81	103.94	101.94	112.47	122.29	133.12	137.12	131.53	141.00	144.71	133.65	123.12
Low controls	24	40.00	40.29	44.79	46.46	52.50	59.29	61.71	60.05	66.71	63.04	56.54	59.00
Public Institutions													
USD recipients	13	90.69	92.31	92.92	98.46	112.08	122.69	130.77	134.38	142.77	142.08	141.00	135.23
DSD recipients	8	49.50	54.50	58.00	66.63	68.63	77.25	92.50	97.13	104.13	104.63	96.88	97.38
High controls	5	211.40	216.20	215.40	219.60	238.20	245.40	252.40	248.20	261.00	261.80	249.40	244.60
Medium controls	13	100.83	115.67	106.75	118.08	127.62	140.62	144.62	137.91	150.08	160.54	141.00	135.46
Low controls	13	38.08	39.69	41.23	46.54	54.46	64.00	65.62	61.50	72.08	66.58	59.62	68.23
Private Institutions													
USD recipients	9	106.56	114.00	64.22	98.67	110.89	111.78	114.78	115.56	108.67	106.44	90.78	78.78
DSD recipients	4	30.75	30.25	34.50	33.50	39.50	43.25	56.00	53.75	28.50	57.00	55.75	56.75
High controls	10	101.30	106.40	113.00	117.70	133.30	136.00	142.40	148.67	156.90	164.50	144.10	146.50
Medium controls	4	72.75	68.75	87.50	94.25	105.00	108.75	112.75	114.00	111.50	93.25	109.75	83.00
Low controls	11	42.27	41.00	49.00	46.36	50.18	53.73	57.09	58.30	60.36	59.18	52.91	48.09

113

TABLE 7-6 Departmental Enrollments in Science Development and Control Institutions: Chemistry (first-year, full-time graduate students only)

	No.	1959	1960	1961	1962	1963	1964	1965	1966	1967	1968	1969	1970
All Institutions													
USD recipients	22	22.10	23.32	25.72	26.00	29.23	34.09	29.32	33.23	29.95	24.32	23.50	23.00
DSD recipients	12	14.67	14.89	14.92	17.75	18.50	22.18	24.36	28.83	25.83	18.67	19.50	23.27
High controls	15	34.53	44.73	39.60	42.27	41.40	44.27	49.73	46.64	49.67	52.67	49.80	43.93
Medium controls	17	16.56	23.00	20.06	26.47	28.06	27.12	35.41	41.80	33.65	36.88	31.65	31.35
Low controls	24	7.75	9.09	10.91	9.79	13.48	13.08	14.96	14.73	17.21	13.14	11.17	14.25
Public Institutions													
USD recipients	13	25.00	26.00	25.92	29.00	35.00	42.54	33.23	36.62	36.69	27.31	29.69	29.00
DSD recipients	8	18.13	16.29	16.63	22.00	22.00	26.38	28.38	35.25	34.88	21.88	22.63	24.75
High controls	5	51.80	70.20	58.40	63.20	52.80	51.60	69.80	57.00	60.80	79.20	79.20	76.40
Medium controls	13	18.08	27.17	20.92	27.31	28.77	28.85	39.69	46.18	37.31	41.85	34.54	34.46
Low controls	13	8.15	10.54	12.17	11.85	16.15	15.38	19.17	14.75	17.46	10.92	10.85	16.69
Private Institutions													
USD recipients	9	18.22	19.44	20.00	21.67	20.89	21.89	23.67	28.33	20.22	20.00	14.56	14.33
DSD recipients	4	7.75	10.00	11.50	9.25	11.50	11.00	13.67	16.00	7.75	12.25	13.25	19.33
High controls	10	25.90	32.00	30.20	31.80	35.70	40.60	39.70	40.89	44.10	39.40	35.10	25.89
Medium controls	4	12.00	10.50	17.50	23.75	25.75	21.50	21.50	29.75	21.75	20.75	22.25	21.25
Low controls	11	7.27	7.20	9.40	7.36	10.00	10.36	10.36	14.70	16.91	15.80	11.60	11.36

114

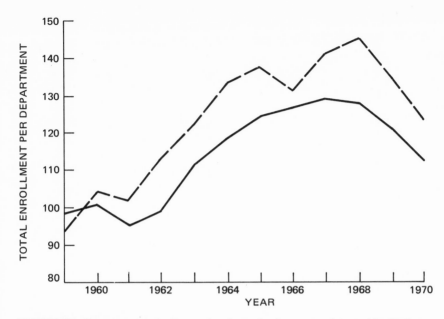

FIGURE 7-7 Departmental enrollments in science development and control institutions (all graduate students): chemistry.

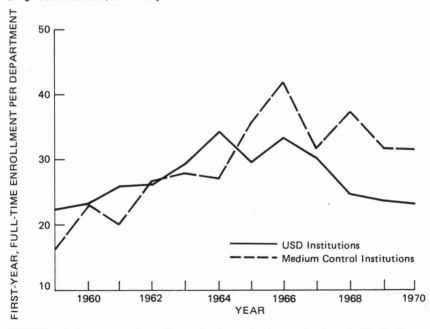

FIGURE 7-8 Departmental enrollments in science development and control institutions (first-year, full-time graduate students only): chemistry.

115

TABLE 7-7 Departmental Enrollments in Science Development and Control Institutions: History (all graduate students)

	No.	1960	1961	1962	1963	1964	1965	1966	1967	1968	1969	1970
All Institutions												
USD recipients	24	79.08	79.79	92.08	106.00	125.04	—	144.46	149.88	149.71	146.42	133.83
High controls	14	162.14	171.79	178.57	197.93	209.64	—	248.77	243.00	260.67	221.07	201.21
Medium controls	18	55.89	63.44	67.50	78.56	89.11	—	109.29	114.47	111.00	122.94	121.44
Low controls	18	55.13	59.29	62.72	67.83	79.00	—	81.28	87.65	79.89	87.59	83.06
Public Institutions												
USD recipients	14	77.86	83.00	100.64	117.86	134.93	—	155.43	162.36	163.64	164.64	164.64
High controls	4	226.25	255.25	276.00	323.50	335.25	—	414.25	417.00	377.00	377.00	359.75
Medium controls	10	58.20	70.50	79.80	95.70	106.90	—	235.60	140.00	129.60	141.50	144.10
Low controls	9	25.43	23.50	35.00	40.67	50.22	—	52.44	63.89	67.22	79.22	76.33
Private Institutions												
USD recipients	10	80.80	75.30	80.10	89.40	111.20	—	129.10	132.40	130.20	120.90	90.70
High controls	10	136.50	138.40	139.60	147.70	159.40	—	175.22	173.40	202.50	158.70	137.80
Medium controls	8	53.00	54.63	52.13	57.13	66.88	—	71.71	78.00	87.75	99.75	93.13
Low controls	9	78.22	91.11	90.44	95.00	111.38	—	110.11	114.38	92.56	97.00	89.78

116

TABLE 7-8 Departmental Enrollments in Science Development and Control Institutions: History (first-year, full-time graduate students only)

	No.	1960	1961	1962	1963	1964	1965	1966	1967	1968	1969	1970
All Institutions												
USD recipients	24	22.71	26.21	30.63	35.08	37.92	—	44.29	51.42	44.67	41.08	37.46
High controls	14	50.79	50.50	49.29	63.36	71.50	—	77.31	65.93	69.08	63.36	56.50
Medium controls	18	17.61	18.28	20.89	24.50	27.50	—	36.18	37.94	31.00	34.33	27.44
Low controls	18	11.50	11.00	15.00	18.00	19.82	—	25.11	21.76	20.12	22.76	24.11
Public Institutions												
USD recipients	14	27.07	30.07	37.14	43.07	47.36	—	54.29	64.21	53.79	52.57	47.21
High controls	4	91.75	83.50	80.50	97.25	97.25	—	121.00	110.50	121.50	126.25	121.00
Medium controls	10	18.90	21.50	27.10	29.80	33.70	—	47.10	49.20	33.40	43.50	35.20
Low controls	9	9.86	8.88	15.89	18.22	18.67	—	23.67	20.22	20.33	26.00	26.56
Private Institutions												
USD recipients	10	16.60	20.80	21.50	23.90	24.70	—	30.30	33.50	31.90	25.00	23.80
High controls	10	34.40	37.30	36.80	49.80	61.20	—	57.89	48.10	42.88	38.20	30.70
Medium controls	8	16.00	14.25	13.13	17.88	19.75	—	20.57	21.86	28.00	22.88	17.75
Low controls	9	12.78	12.89	14.11	17.78	21.13	—	26.56	23.50	19.88	19.13	21.67

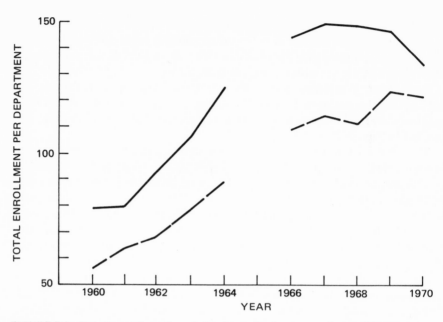

FIGURE 7-9 Departmental enrollments in science development and control institutions (all graduate students): history.

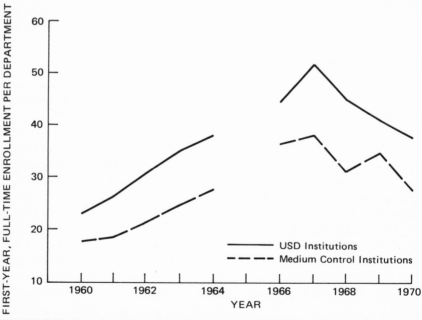

FIGURE 7-10 Departmental enrollments in science development and control institutions (first-year, full-time graduate students only): history.

118

ment level and a dummy variable indicating whether or not the school got a grant; the second partial is between enrollment level and total departmental science funding (as measured in 1968). Both partials were computed after all predictor variables were controlled for.

Each year a residual score was computed for each institution by subtracting the estimated enrollment from the actual enrollment. These residuals, averaged for both the experimental and the control groups, are plotted in Figure 7-11.

In Table 7-10 and Figure 7-12 information on the results of a similar analyses with respect to first-year full-time enrollments is presented.

The multivariate analysis leads to some interesting conclusions. In mathematics both the pattern of partial correlations and the residual plots indicate an effect of funding on first-year enrollments. In physics this seems true for both total and first-year enrollments; however, the gap between the USD and control residual curves is seen as early as 1965, an indication that factors other than the NSF program may be at work. The residual analysis shows no impact in either chemistry or history.[1]

In short, while the zero-order analyses revealed little impact of the funding on either first-year or total graduate enrollments (with the exception of public institutions in mathematics), the multivariate analyses show an impact on first-year enrollments in math and, possibly, on both enrollment indices in physics.

EFFECTS ON GRADUATE STUDENT QUALITY

The analyses reported above, while necessary, dealt with the *quantity,* not the *quality,* of graduate students. Since Science Development aimed at improving the *quality* of science at the recipient institutions, also the focus of this evaluative study, additional analyses were conducted using two indicators of the quality of entering graduate students: (1) scores on the Graduate Record Examination (a standardized test of aptitude, with a verbal and a quantitative component) and (2) the selectivity levels of students' baccalaureate institutions.

Obtaining information on GRE test scores proved to be quite a difficult task. The Educational Testing Service (ETS) has these data, but they are neither organized by, nor contain information about, the graduate school at which an applicant subsequently enrolls. Thus, to discover the average GRE score of students entering, say, the graduate chemistry department at the University of Michigan two steps were required. First, we contacted

[1] The rather large partial correlations for history are intriguing. They probably indicate the observation made earlier that schools receiving USD grants had larger first-year enrollments before, during, and after the funding.

TABLE 7-9 Prediction of Total Enrollments, 1965–1970

	1965	1966	1967	1968	1969	1970
Mathematics (N = 65)						
Multiple correlation	0.54	0.62	0.63	0.48	0.47	0.62
Regression coefficients[a]						
Faculty size	0.30	0.36	0.33	0.24	0.25	0.31
Doctorate production	−0.09	−0.09	−0.09	−0.24	−0.16	−0.11
Publication rates	0.25	0.30	0.45	0.35	0.25	0.44
Science funding to university	0.15	0.12	0.01	0.16	0.18	0.04
Partial correlation[b]						
Science development grant	0.04	0.11	0.13	0.03	0.08	0.12
All federal funds to department	0.07	0.08	0.05	0.18	0.22	0.07
Chemistry (N = 87)						
Multiple correlation	0.86	0.80	0.87	0.85	0.84	0.85
Regression coefficients[a]						
Faculty size	0.10	0.22	0.11	0.11	0.23	0.16
Doctorate production	0.88	0.74	0.59	0.62	0.48	0.50
Publication rates	0.04	−0.20	0.31	0.23	0.24	0.24
Science funding to university	−0.19	0.08	−0.14	−0.10	−0.08	0.01
Partial correlation[b]						
Science development grant	0.14	0.26	0.14	0.18	0.19	0.16
All federal funds to department						

Physics (N = 82)						
Multiple correlation	0.77	0.77	0.78	0.70	0.80	0.72
Regression coefficients[a]						
Faculty size	0.11	0.16	0.23	0.17	0.21	0.19
Doctorate production	0.28	0.10	0.34	0.25	0.02	0.16
Publication rates	0.24	0.27	0.08	0.17	0.34	0.27
Science funding to university	0.21	0.32	0.21	0.20	0.33	0.19
Partial correlation[b]						
Science development grant	0.20	0.28	0.31	0.26	0.30	0.27
All federal funds to department	−0.11	−0.06	−0.11	−0.06	−0.01	0.13
History (N = 72)						
Multiple correlation		0.72	0.72	0.68	0.67	0.67
Regression coefficients[a]						
Faculty size		0.35	0.30	0.28	0.27	0.32
Doctorate production		0.47	0.53	0.53	0.41	0.35
Publication rates		−0.45	−0.48	−0.45	−0.41	−0.34
Science funding to university		0.39	0.41	0.37	0.44	0.39
Partial correlation[b]						
Science development grant		0.20	0.22	0.24	0.18	0.13

[a] Regression coefficients are standardized.
[b] Partials controlled for the four variables above.

121

TABLE 7-10 Prediction of First-Year Graduate Enrollments, 1965-1970

	1965	1966	1967	1968	1969	1970
Mathematics ($N = 65$)						
Multiple correlation	0.58	0.62	0.57	0.58	0.62	0.63
Regression coefficients[a]						
Faculty size	0.48	0.51	0.39	0.31	0.32	0.24
Doctorate production	-0.05	-0.08	0.07	0.05	0.03	0.04
Publication rates	0.08	0.04	0.19	0.37	0.28	0.52
Science funding to university	0.12	0.21	0.00	-0.07	0.07	-0.11
Partial correlation[b]						
Science development grant	0.13	0.07	0.13	0.17	0.23	0.14
All federal funds to department	-0.06	0.02	0.12	-0.05	0.00	-0.14
Chemistry ($N = 87$)						
Multiple correlation	0.70	0.58	0.63	0.69	0.71	0.74
Regression coefficients[a]						
Faculty size	0.28	0.13	0.06	-0.04	-0.01	0.13
Doctorate production	0.57	0.65	0.45	0.20	0.36	0.53
Publication rates	-0.15	-0.20	0.25	0.57	0.45	0.08
Science funding to university	0.06	0.01	-0.14	-0.05	-0.08	0.05
Partial correlation[b]						
Science development grant	0.05	0.17	0.10	-0.00	0.03	0.00
All federal funds to department	0.11	0.17				

Physics (N = 82)

Multiple correlation	0.58	0.63	0.66	0.63	0.72	0.56
Regression coefficients[a]						
Faculty size	0.13	0.32	0.40	0.19	0.25	0.09
Doctorate production	0.01	-0.01	0.06	-0.10	-0.17	0.18
Publication rates	0.12	0.04	0.10	0.49	0.56	0.35
Science funding to university	0.38	0.36	0.18	0.12	0.16	-0.03
Partial correlation[b]						
Science development grant	0.18	0.29	0.32	0.20	0.26	0.24
All federal funds to department	-0.21	-0.01	-0.11	-0.29	-0.19	-0.21

History (N = 72)

Multiple correlation		0.68	0.53	0.55	0.61	0.58
Regression coefficients[a]						
Faculty size		0.27	0.21	0.28	0.31	0.25
Doctorate production		0.56	0.56	0.27	0.01	-0.00
Publication rates		-0.50	-0.40	-0.27	-0.19	-0.20
Science funding to university		0.37	0.17	0.30	0.50	0.54
Partial correlation[b]						
Science development grant		0.20	0.33	0.24	0.09	0.09

[a] Regression coefficients are standardized.
[b] Partials controlled for the four variables above.

123

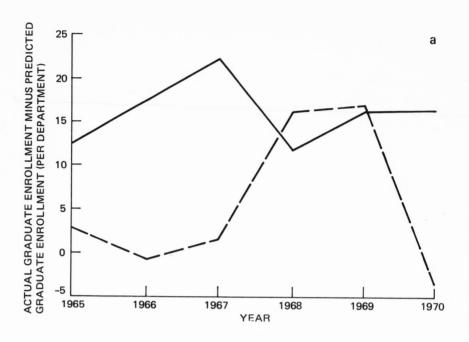

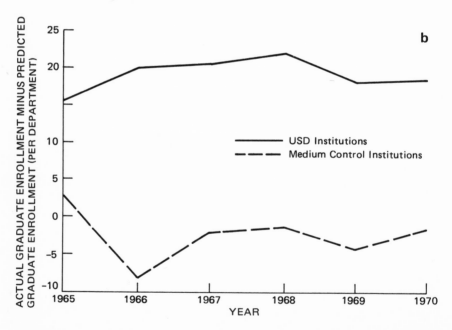

FIGURE 7-11 Residual analysis of total graduate enrollments: (a) mathematics, (b) physics, (c) chemistry, (d) history.

124

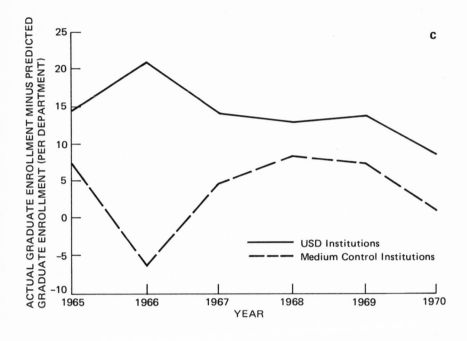

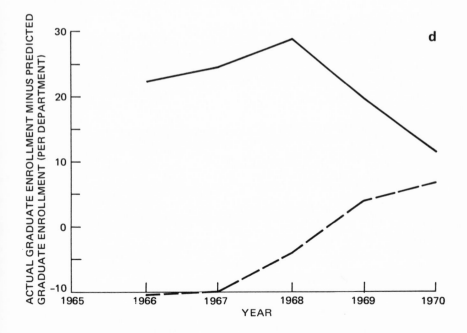

125

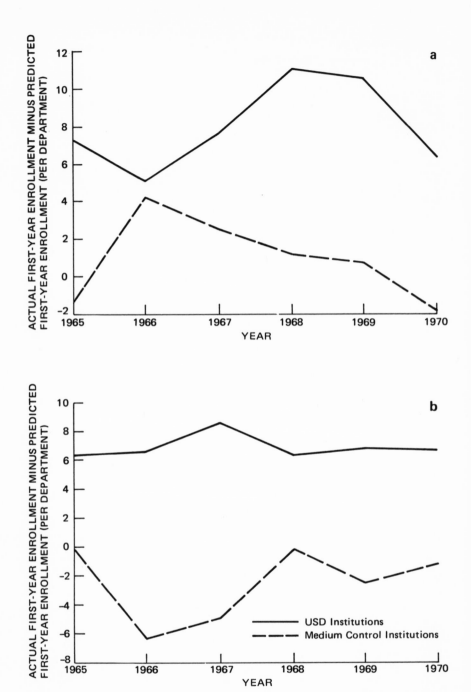

FIGURE 7-12   Residual analysis of first-year, full-time graduate enrollments: (a) mathematics, (b) physics, (c) chemistry, (d) history.

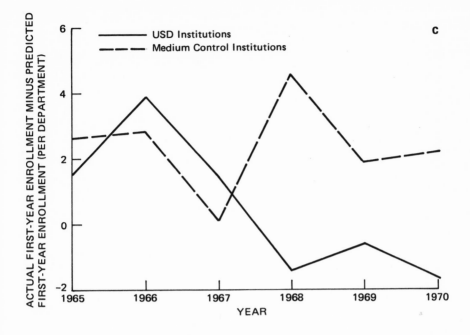

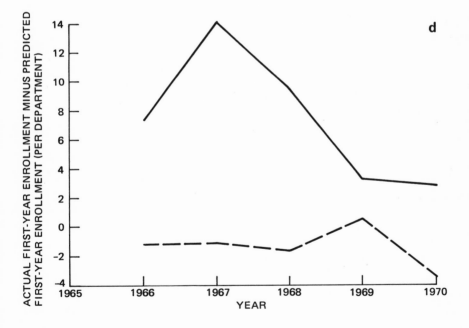

127

TABLE 7-11 Average Graduate Record Examination Scores in Science Development and Control Institutions, 1964 and 1973

	All Institutions				Public				Private			
	1964		1973		1964		1973		1964		1973	
	No. Students	Score	No. Students	Score	No. Students	Score	No. Students	Score	No. Students	Score	No. Students	Score
Chemistry												
Verbal												
USD	184	554.50	239	527.87	139	557.92	166	542.45	45	543.93	73	494.70
DSD	33	516.48	98	496.31	23	519.74	73	477.81	10	509.00	25	550.32
High	88	611.66	290	581.63	15	561.00	79	552.00	73	622.07	211	592.73
Medium	79	563.49	195	504.75	52	546.46	136	503.43	29	596.30	59	507.81
Low	78	543.60	75	473.81	60	521.95	39	462.49	18	615.78	36	486.08
Quantitative												
USD	184	641.57	239	669.85	139	639.43	166	676.80	45	648.18	73	654.05
DSD	33	643.45	98	633.77	23	650.61	73	622.49	10	627.00	25	666.68
High	88	698.83	290	703.00	15	678.00	79	699.57	73	703.11	211	704.28
Medium	79	655.38	195	660.34	52	654.23	136	662.88	27	686.85	59	654.49
Low	78	620.22	75	633.11	60	617.58	39	634.49	18	629.00	36	631.61
History												
Verbal												
USD	185	591.33	270	610.08	119	584.29	184	612.35	66	604.02	86	604.64
High	118	690.36	204	668.27	0	0.00	0	0.00	118	690.36	204	668.27
Medium	115	598.10	165	613.97	65	576.34	83	600.95	50	626.38	82	627.15
Low	30	548.40	99	597.75	18	529.67	45	555.36	12	576.50	54	633.07
Quantitative												
USD	185	533.89	270	556.12	119	539.60	184	558.04	66	523.59	86	551.52
High	118	604.20	204	591.68	0	0.00	0	0.00	118	604.20	204	591.68
Medium	115	535.56	165	524.93	65	535.85	83	512.52	50	535.21	82	537.50
Low	30	490.60	99	514.78	18	506.94	45	494.89	12	466.08	54	531.35

each graduate department and asked for a list of graduate students who had entered in a given year. Second, we sent this list to ETS, which retrieved the test scores for each student and then averaged the scores over the department.[2]

Because of the considerable complexity and cost of the retrieval process, it was necessary to limit both the number of fields and the years examined. Thus, in March 1974, following a pretest of the retrieval instrument, a request was sent to all Roose–Andersen-rated chemistry and history departments asking them to list all students entering their departments in the fall of 1964 and the fall of 1973. (The letter was addressed to the graduate dean, who in many cases forwarded it to the department chairmen. In short, the location of the appropriate data within the university varied from institution to institution.) In addition, the departments were asked to indicate, where possible, each student's baccalaureate institution and (verbal and quantitative) GRE score. Most institutions were unable to provide GRE data, either because of data retrieval problems or considerations of confidentiality. Finally, the departments were asked to indicate the birthdate of each student for whom GRE data were not provided in order to facilitate communications with ETS.

Several reminder letters were sent to the nonresponding departments. Ultimately, 78 percent of the chemistry departments answered the request and provided some or all information, as did 79 percent of the history departments. In light of the haphazard recordkeeping of many universities, we offered to reimburse each department for any significant clerical time involved in retrieving this information. Few responding departments found it necessary to draw upon this resource.

The names of the students whose test scores were not provided by the institution were then forwarded to ETS. The information sent back by ETS for each department indicated the number of students whose test scores they were able to retrieve and the mean verbal and quantitative scores of the graduate students in that department. At no time did they provide data on the test scores of individual students.

Table 7-11 presents the results of these analyses, indicating both "before" and "after" GRE (verbal and quantitative) aptitude scores in the funded field of chemistry and the control field of history for each of the five

[2] Lincoln Moses, a member of both the Study Advisory Panel and the Graduate Record Examination Board, helped us negotiate this arrangement with ETS. The Project Officer at ETS was Mr. J. Martin Glaubitz. In the process of obtaining these mean GRE scores per department, rules of strict confidentiality were observed by both the study and ETS. Specifically, no individual test scores were used in the analyses reported in this chapter, nor were they retained on any data files. The Educational Testing Service was sent a list of names and responded with a mean score for each department but did not supply the study with the scores of individuals.

groups of institutions. Science Development funding seems to have significantly affected the quality of the students entering recipient departments. In chemistry the change in scores on both the verbal and quantitative components of the GRE for students entering the recipient departments was much better than that experienced by students entering control departments.[3] The quantitative scores of the former group increased while it decreased for the latter; scores on the verbal component declined for both groups but the decline was much smaller for students entering funded schools. These differences and trends were seen in both the public and private sector. In history the changes in verbal GRE scores for both groups between 1964 and 1973 were similar. However, the quantitative scores of students entering history departments at recipient schools increased while those of students entering control departments decreased.

In short, there seems to be an effect of Science Development funding on the GRE scores of students entering recipient chemistry departments. However, the findings from history suggest that the changes on the quantitative component of the test may be a result of other institutional changes.

Since GRE data had only been available for a prefunding and a postfunding year, it was not possible to use the same multivariate analysis techniques as were employed with the other variables. Multiple regressions, however, were run and partial correlations computed in a manner analogous to that used by the author in his assessment of the effects of the NSF College Science Improvement program on undergraduates.[4] That is, two regressions were run in chemistry predicting both the verbal and the quantitative GRE score in 1973. In each case the predictors were the 1964 pretest on that variable and prefunding measures of doctoral production, faculty size, publication rate, graduate enrollment and federal science

[3] In computing these figures, the differing sample sizes affecting the departmental means were taken into account. A weighted sum, computed for each of the groups was divided by the total number of students entering departments in that group. The process was not to average the separate department means (which were based on widely differing numbers.)

One potentially complicating factor should be noted. The ability of either the schools or ETS to retrieve data on students varied considerably from department to department as a function of whether or not the department required this test. Clearly, the students who entered departments that did not require the test but who took it anyway constitute a special, biased subset of students. As an additional complication, the number of departments requiring the GRE changed between 1964 and 1973.

The key difference—between the 1973 USD and medium control verbal scores for chemistry departments—is statistically significant, assuming that the standard deviation of the scores is 125 (the figure provided by ETS). In point of fact, the actual σ for these students probably is smaller in light of their homogeneity, a fact which would increase the strength of the finding.

[4] David E. Drew, *A Study of the NSF College Science Improvement Program*, ACE Research Reports, Vol. 6, No. 4, (Washington: American Council on Education, 1971.)

funding to the institution. The multiple correlation for the two equations were 0.35 (verbal) and 0.38 (quantitative). A partial correlation was computed between each criterion variable and a dummy variable indicating whether or not the department received a Science Development grant (while controlling for all predictor variables). For the verbal scores the partial correlation was 0.31; the quantitative measure, 0.18. These results, then, reinforce the zero order finding about the effect of funding on graduate student aptitudes, particularly when contrasted with history where the corresponding partial correlations were −0.28 and 0.08, respectively.

Our other measure of the quality of graduate students was the kind of undergraduate college from which they graduated. As described above,

TABLE 7-12   Baccalaureate Origins of Students Entering Science Development and Control Departments, 1964 and 1973

	No.	Number of Students		Average Selectivity Score[a]	
		1964	1973	1964	1973
All Institutions					
Chemistry					
USD	16	350	231	1087.55	1072.99
Medium controls	14	321	259	1085.65	1063.88
History					
USD	14	366	219	1092.78	1090.42
Medium controls	9	175	131	1077.90	1103.87
Public Institutions					
Chemistry					
USD	9	237	164	1081.92	1057.63
Medium controls	11	261	217	1070.11	1056.81
History					
USD	5	192	138	1063.49	1082.05
Medium controls	4	84	61	1056.05	1057.61
Private Institutions					
Chemistry					
USD	7	113	67	1099.35	1108.18
Medium controls	3	60	42	1153.25	1100.40
History					
USD	9	174	81	1125.09	1104.68
Medium controls	5	91	70	1098.08	1144.19

[a] Average selectivity (combined verbal plus quantitative SAT score) of the students' undergraduate colleges.

131

information about the school of baccalaureate origin for students entering chemistry and history departments in 1973 and 1964 was collected directly from the universities. Each undergraduate college was coded with a selectivity measure based on the average aptitude test scores of its entering freshman.[5] These undergraduate selectivity scores were then averaged over the experimental and control groups. The results from these calculations are presented in Table 7-12. Data are presented on both Science Development and control institutions for both the pre- and postfunding years in chemistry and in history. The information is summarized for all institutions, public institutions only, and private institutions.

Inspection of this table reveals no startling differences between the behavior of the USD and the control departments in the funded field of chemistry, with the possible exception of the private sector. Here the selectivity score of students entering funded departments increased slightly at the same time that the score of students entering the control departments dropped considerably. Perhaps the most interesting observation about this table is how little the baccalaureate selectivity level of students entering these departments changed between 1964 and 1973.

[5] Alexander W. Astin, *Predicting Academic Performance in College: Selectivity Data for 2300 American Colleges,* (New York: The Free Press, A Division of the Macmillan Company, 1971.)

8 Impact on the Production of Doctorates

The dawn of the 1970s saw graduate education enter a period of crisis. For over a decade, the expansionary thrust of university research had been bolstered by increasing amounts of federal support; in the early 1970s, this federal support leveled off under the Nixon administration. Concomitantly, other traditional sources of revenue became reluctant to support graduate education because of a highly publicized surplus of Ph.D.s. One of the primary topics considered by the National Board on Graduate Education in its initial statement was this overproduction of Ph.D.s.[1]

A facile criticism sometimes leveled at the Science Development program is that it was the right program at the wrong time: i.e., that its main effect was to create Ph.D.s who subsequently had difficulty finding employment. In light of the salience of this issue to graduate education in general, and to Science Development in particular, a special set of analyses was devoted to examining the effects of Science Development funding on Ph.D. production and to tracing the subsequent employment of Ph.D.s from schools that received funding.

In the mid-1960s, national support for graduate education was at its height, and most experts were predicting a shortage of Ph.D.s through the next decade. Economist Allan Cartter, however, took a somewhat different view, reporting that his analyses and projections indicated that the future demand for Ph.Ds would not be likely to exceed the supply. As a

---

[1] National Board on Graduate Education, *Graduate Education: Purposes, Problems, and Potential,* (Washington: National Academy of Sciences, 1972).

partial explanation of the differences between his conclusions and those of other specialists, Cartter noted that "educational researchers in government agencies had collected the wrong information for many years and had drawn hasty conclusions from imperfect data."[2] Continuing his analysis in subsequent articles, Cartter was one of the first, if not the first, to predict an oversupply of Ph.D.s beginning in the 1970s. For example, in 1972, he stated: "We are on a course which would result in one-third too many Ph.D.s produced in the latter part of this decade and perhaps one-half too many in the 1980s for the types of employment we have known in the past."[3]

In light of the accuracy of his early projections, Cartter's work has received a good deal of attention. But he is not without his critics. For example, Vaughn and Sjoberg have questioned some of Cartter's assumptions and given a number of reasons for viewing his projections with some skepticism. They charge that Cartter "ignores fundamental social changes already underway within American society, changes that are likely to erode the very basis of his projections."[4] Essentially, they argue that basic shifts in the nature of the American economy will lead a larger number of people to seek higher education than Cartter had assumed. The emerging primacy of the service sector in the economy implies a greater reliance on advanced education, as does the increase in leisure time and the growing demands of women, minorities, and others for advanced education on a part- or full-time basis.

While national policymakers have been slowly sifting and developing an approach to this problem, a number of states have taken direct action. Foremost among these is New York, where the State Board of Regents is invested with considerable authority over both public and private education. A recent report recommended that the number of doctoral-producing programs be reduced, citing, among other factors, the overproduction of Ph.D.s by the state's higher education institutions.[5] A special study has been commissioned to review and evaluate, on a field-by-field basis, the adequacy of doctoral programs and to make recommendations about which should be abolished and which strengthened.

The growth of graduate education during the 1960s occurred at different rates in different sectors of the academic world. For example, as Kidd has

---

[2] Allan M. Cartter, "A New Look at the Supply of College Teachers," *Educational Record,* Vol. 46, Summer, 1965, pp. 267-277.

[3] Allan M. Cartter, "Scientific Manpower of 1970–85," *Science,* April 9, 1972, p. 243.

[4] Ted R. Vaughan and Gideon Sjoberg, "The Politics of Projection: A Critique of Cartter's Analysis," *Science,* July 14, 1972, p. 142.

[5] "Meeting the Needs of Doctoral Education in New York State," New York Board of Regents, Commission of Doctoral Education, Albany, New York, January, 1973.

noted, over the decade doctoral production in the top 30 private universities dropped from 39 percent to 27 percent of the total of all doctorates produced, whereas in the public universities below the top 30, it increased from 9 percent to 24 percent. These percentage changes are set against a background in which overall Ph.D. production tripled between 1960 (10,000) and 1969 (30,000). Among the reasons Kidd notes for the differential growth rates of different types of institutions are the steep increases in state budgets for support of state institutions in the sixties, the greater expansion of public universities in every aspect, and the pressure to provide teaching assistants for the rapidly growing undergraduate population at public universities.[6]

Observations such as these about the differential growth rates of public and private institutions have led some observers[7] to argue that Ph.D. output should be limited, essentially to elite institutions. Obviously, this reasoning runs counter to the philosophical considerations that led to the creation of the Science Development program.

Clearly, the impact of Science Development funds on Ph.D. production and the resulting implications for manpower must be examined carefully in a study such as this. But it must not be forgotten that factors other than simply manpower considerations should affect the development of higher education institutions. For example, Kidd notes that plans for the future of graduate education must take into account the needs of society and the needs of individuals.[8] Similarly, a National Board on Graduate Education statement listed three basic models for studying these issues—manpower planning, human capital, free student choice—and endorsed the third:

Graduate education is more than investment in human capital and more than a means to train people for specific jobs, although it includes both of these. We support the principle of free choice for students and believe that it would be a serious error in public policy to close off opportunities to potential graduate students on the basis of a centralized manpower plan, or because the "investment" may not return the market rate of interest.[9]

Thus, our use of Ph.D. production as a key index of quality is justified in that this measure is closely related both to current controversies in graduate education and to a key criticism of the Science Development

[6] Charles V. Kidd, "Shifts in Doctoral Output: History and Outlook," *Science*, February 9, 1973 pp. 538–543.
[7] John R. Niland, "Allocation of Ph.D. Manpower in the Academic Labor Market," *Industrial Relations*, Vol. 11, No. 2, May, 1972 pp. 141–156.
[8] Charles V. Kidd, "Doctorate Ouptut—Over Production or Under Consumption," (Speech delivered to the American Association for Higher Education, March 13, 1973.)
[9] National Board on Graduate Education, *Doctorate Manpower Forecasts and Policy*, No. 2 (Washington: National Academy of Sciences, 1973), p. 5.

program. Some observers, of course, consider Ph.D. production to be a basic indication of graduate quality. For example, Cartter used a measure of doctorate production as the key criterion for inclusion of schools and programs to be assessed in his ratings; Roose and Andersen, in their replication of his study, followed this lead. In this chapter, then, the rates of Ph.D. production in Science Development and in control institutions are compared. This is followed by an analysis of first jobs acquired by recent graduates in both the academic world and industry.

TRENDS IN DOCTORATE PRODUCTION

This analysis of trends in Ph.D. production was based on the Doctorate Record File produced annually by the National Research Council (NRC). Each year since 1958 the NRC has conducted a census of all graduating Ph.D.s. Each doctorate recipient completes a four-page questionnaire. The samples from these surveys are virtually complete: i.e., the response rates are between 99 and 100 percent. While the questionnaires provide a rich body of data, the major focus in these analyses was on a simple head count of the number of Ph.D.s produced.

Data from the Doctorate Record File for the 15-year period, 1958 through 1972, were collected and analyzed. As before, the emphasis was on comparing five analytic groups of institutions: USD recipients, DSD recipients, high controls, medium controls, and low controls. The findings reported below are derived from the examination of the three major science fields—physics, chemistry, and mathematics—and the control field of history.

Of course, in comparing Science Development and control institutions on a primary variable such as Ph.D. production, one must bear in mind the national trends. In Figure 8-1 the number of doctorates produced in each of the four fields over the 15-year period is plotted. In each field the total number of doctorates produced by all institutions in the sample, whether experimental or control, are combined. As the graph shows, doctorate production rose steadily through the sixties, peaked in 1970, and has tapered off slightly since. This finding holds true for each field and reflects the crisis situation in graduate education that touched off the debate of the past few years. That is, the tapering-off after the rapid ascent can be seen as the system's adjustment to reductions in federal support and to the surplus of Ph.D.s.

Tables 8-1 to 8-4 present the results of the analysis of Ph.D. production for each field. The average number of doctorates per institution for each of the five groups is given for each year separately for all institutions, public only, and private only.

136

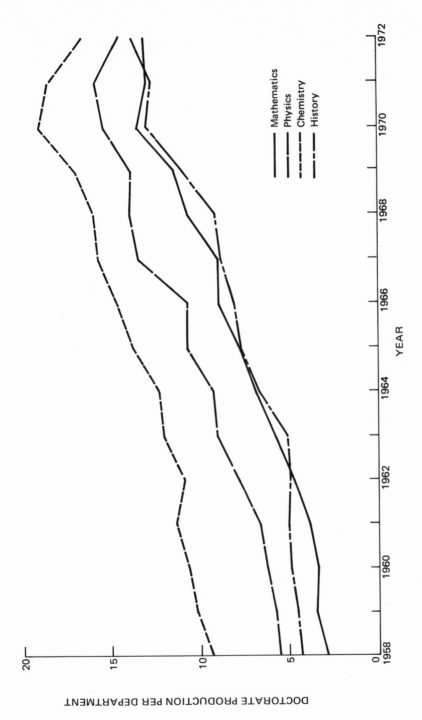

FIGURE 8-1 Overall trends in doctorate production by field (all major institutions).

137

TABLE 8-1 Doctorate Production In Science Development and Control Institutions: Mathematics

	No.	1958	1959	1960	1961	1962	1963	1964	1965	1966	1967	1968	1969	1970	1971	1972
All Institutions																
USD recipients	15	1.80	2.07	2.27	2.40	2.87	3.20	5.47	4.47	6.27	6.93	7.47	8.67	12.40	10.87	9.20
DSD recipients	5	0.40	0.20	0.40	0.80	0.80	1.00	1.60	1.60	1.40	2.40	4.40	5.80	6.60	4.20	6.80
High controls	17	6.71	8.06	8.18	8.76	11.29	13.47	16.29	17.82	20.24	19.29	22.29	22.12	25.12	24.47	26.06
Medium controls	15	1.53	2.40	1.73	1.67	2.73	4.00	3.93	5.20	6.00	6.40	7.33	9.53	10.13	10.73	10.13
Low controls	16	1.13	1.38	1.50	2.31	1.88	2.06	2.00	3.25	3.50	3.31	4.81	4.31	4.94	5.13	5.31
Public Institutions																
USD recipients	9	1.56	2.22	2.89	2.56	2.78	3.22	5.00	6.00	7.44	7.00	8.00	10.11	13.22	12.33	10.44
DSD recipients	2	1.00	0.0	0.50	1.50	1.00	1.50	2.00	2.00	1.00	4.50	6.50	10.00	10.50	6.50	10.50
High controls	6	7.67	8.50	10.67	9.67	14.00	19.00	19.67	22.67	24.50	25.83	31.00	30.00	33.83	34.67	32.17
Medium controls	8	1.75	2.13	2.00	2.13	2.38	5.63	4.38	6.38	5.75	6.00	7.25	9.63	10.25	10.50	9.13
Low controls	10	1.10	0.90	1.20	2.60	2.00	2.80	2.50	3.70	4.90	4.00	5.60	5.40	5.90	5.20	5.80
Private Institutions																
USD recipients	6	2.17	1.83	1.33	2.17	3.00	3.17	6.17	2.17	4.50	6.83	6.67	6.50	11.17	8.67	7.33
DSD recipients	3	0.0	0.33	0.33	0.33	0.67	0.67	1.33	1.33	1.67	1.00	3.00	3.00	4.00	2.67	4.33
High controls	11	6.18	7.82	6.82	8.27	9.82	10.45	14.45	15.18	17.91	15.73	17.55	17.82	20.36	18.91	22.73
Medium controls	7	1.29	2.71	1.43	1.14	3.14	2.14	3.43	3.86	6.29	6.86	7.43	9.43	10.00	11.00	11.29
Low controls	6	1.17	2.17	2.00	1.83	1.67	0.83	1.17	2.50	1.17	2.17	3.50	2.50	3.33	5.00	4.50

TABLE 8-2 Doctorate Production in Science Development and Control Institutions: Physics

	No.	1958	1959	1960	1961	1962	1963	1964	1965	1966	1967	1968	1969	1970	1971	1972
All Institutions																
USD recipients	25	5.12	5.08	5.36	5.60	6.00	7.68	9.00	9.36	9.68	10.40	13.76	13.52	14.72	15.48	14.24
DSD recipients	9	1.00	0.78	1.89	1.22	2.22	4.00	3.33	4.33	4.67	6.56	7.11	5.56	9.00	9.56	8.11
High controls	14	14.29	16.07	16.21	17.79	22.93	24.14	22.71	26.29	26.36	34.43	30.71	30.43	32.71	37.00	31.64
Medium controls	18	4.78	4.00	4.61	5.61	6.17	6.56	6.83	9.00	9.11	11.78	10.78	11.56	12.89	12.83	11.61
Low controls	19	0.84	1.63	1.47	1.84	2.00	2.32	2.79	3.53	2.42	4.21	4.16	4.42	6.16	4.47	4.74
Public Institutions																
USD recipients	16	4.19	4.88	4.81	4.94	5.63	8.31	8.25	10.19	9.94	10.38	14.44	15.19	15.75	15.13	15.75
DSD recipients	6	1.50	1.17	2.33	1.17	2.83	4.33	2.50	4.00	4.00	7.00	7.00	5.83	8.67	9.50	9.33
High controls	4	15.75	14.75	17.75	22.25	27.50	24.00	28.50	26.00	31.75	40.00	36.25	33.50	37.00	39.25	31.50
Medium controls	8	4.38	3.75	4.75	6.25	6.38	7.88	7.38	9.13	8.88	13.13	11.63	12.00	12.75	16.88	14.63
Low controls	13	0.77	1.85	1.92	2.46	2.00	2.69	3.38	4.46	3.00	5.08	5.00	5.00	7.31	5.31	5.62
Private Institutions																
USD recipients	9	6.78	5.44	6.33	6.78	6.67	6.56	10.33	7.89	9.22	10.44	12.56	10.56	12.89	16.11	11.56
DSD recipients	3	0.0	0.0	1.00	1.33	1.00	3.33	5.00	5.00	6.00	5.67	7.33	5.00	9.67	9.67	5.67
High controls	10	13.70	16.60	15.60	16.00	21.10	24.20	20.40	26.40	24.20	32.20	28.50	29.20	31.00	36.10	31.70
Medium controls	10	5.10	4.20	4.50	5.10	6.00	5.50	6.40	8.90	9.30	10.70	10.10	11.20	13.00	9.60	9.20
Low controls	6	1.00	1.17	0.50	0.50	2.00	1.50	1.50	1.50	1.17	2.33	2.33	3.17	3.67	2.67	2.83

139

TABLE 8-3 Doctorate Production in Science Development and Control Institutions: Chemistry

	No.	1958	1959	1960	1961	1962	1963	1964	1965	1966	1967	1968	1969	1970	1971	1972
All Institutions																
USD recipients	22	8.64	10.05	9.05	10.05	11.50	12.00	12.41	13.09	14.00	15.27	15.64	16.36	19.50	18.41	18.14
DSD recipients	12	4.42	4.50	4.42	6.33	5.25	5.42	6.42	7.00	9.50	8.17	9.92	11.17	12.58	12.75	9.67
High controls	15	21.80	21.13	25.27	24.13	23.67	25.80	25.40	27.87	28.47	31.27	31.07	33.27	33.80	33.80	29.13
Medium controls	17	10.88	11.71	12.47	14.41	12.29	14.53	15.35	16.71	18.59	18.94	19.53	20.59	23.24	22.06	20.35
Low controls	24	3.00	3.88	3.38	3.08	3.25	3.79	3.17	5.04	4.75	6.38	5.83	6.83	8.42	7.75	6.50
Public Institutions																
USD recipients	13	7.92	9.23	7.31	10.23	12.23	11.54	12.69	13.31	15.54	16.92	17.46	18.38	20.85	20.15	21.31
DSD recipients	8	5.00	5.13	4.88	6.25	5.75	6.00	7.88	8.13	11.38	9.25	9.88	12.38	15.13	14.38	12.13
High controls	5	32.60	31.20	36.40	33.40	34.00	34.40	32.40	39.20	40.20	43.20	43.80	48.20	47.60	41.40	37.00
Medium controls	13	12.15	12.23	12.62	15.69	12.85	15.62	16.23	17.54	20.08	20.15	21.46	21.31	23.46	23.77	22.23
Low controls	13	2.54	4.38	3.77	2.54	3.46	4.15	2.92	5.46	5.00	7.62	5.85	7.23	9.08	9.15	8.15
Private Institutions																
USD recipients	9	9.67	11.22	11.56	9.78	10.44	12.67	12.00	12.78	11.78	12.89	13.00	13.44	17.56	15.89	13.56
DSD recipients	4	3.25	3.25	3.50	6.50	4.25	4.25	3.50	4.75	5.75	6.00	10.00	8.75	7.50	9.50	4.75
High controls	10	16.40	16.10	19.70	19.50	18.50	21.50	21.90	22.20	22.60	25.30	24.70	25.80	26.90	30.00	25.20
Medium controls	4	6.75	10.00	12.00	10.25	10.50	11.00	12.50	14.00	13.75	15.00	13.25	18.25	22.50	16.50	14.25
Low controls	11	3.55	3.27	2.91	3.73	3.00	3.36	3.45	4.55	4.45	4.91	5.82	6.36	7.64	6.09	4.55

TABLE 8-4 Doctorate Production in Science Development and Control Institutions: History

	No.	1958	1959	1960	1961	1962	1963	1964	1965	1966	1967	1968	1969	1970	1971	1972
All Institutions																
USD recipients	24	3.00	2.96	3.17	3.54	3.96	4.46	6.04	7.42	6.58	7.75	7.71	10.00	12.42	11.50	14.21
High controls	14	11.36	11.36	14.00	12.93	12.57	12.36	17.57	18.36	19.86	21.07	20.07	25.71	31.07	27.21	27.79
Medium controls	18	2.89	3.39	2.94	3.78	2.89	2.78	3.67	4.50	5.33	7.11	6.61	6.89	7.67	8.94	9.11
Low controls	18	1.44	1.83	1.50	1.94	1.89	2.22	2.28	3.00	3.39	2.94	4.67	4.56	4.22	6.06	5.44
Public Institutions																
USD recipients	14	3.50	2.29	3.71	3.71	4.29	4.57	6.07	7.00	6.71	8.43	7.93	10.43	13.00	12.21	14.50
High controls	4	7.25	11.25	14.00	14.50	11.25	12.00	16.25	20.25	22.00	23.00	22.75	31.25	43.25	36.25	36.50
Medium controls	10	3.80	4.00	3.30	4.60	3.50	3.60	4.20	4.90	5.70	9.20	7.10	9.30	9.30	11.10	10.60
Low controls	9	0.33	0.22	0.11	0.89	1.22	1.11	1.11	1.67	2.11	1.56	2.33	3.22	3.11	4.22	3.00
Private Institutions																
USD recipients	10	2.30	3.90	2.40	3.30	3.50	4.30	6.00	8.00	6.40	6.80	7.40	9.40	11.60	10.50	13.80
High controls	10	13.00	11.40	14.00	12.30	13.10	12.50	18.10	17.60	19.00	20.30	19.00	23.50	26.20	23.60	24.30
Medium controls	8	1.75	2.63	2.50	2.75	2.13	1.75	3.00	4.00	4.88	4.50	6.00	3.88	5.63	6.25	7.25
Low controls	9	2.56	3.44	2.89	3.00	2.56	3.33	3.44	4.33	4.67	4.33	7.00	5.89	5.33	7.89	7.89

141

Several interesting trends emerge. The most pertinent comparison, of course, is between the USD recipients and the medium controls in each field. These data are plotted in Figures 8-2 through 8-5.

The impact of Science Development funds on Ph.D. production in mathematics seems negligible; the only postfunding point at which the recipient group greatly exceeded the control group was in 1970. However, further inspection revealed striking differences between the trends in the public and private domain. The data from the public sector appears to indicate that Science Development funds influenced the production of doctorates among these universities; in the private sector the opposite trend is seen, i.e., the controls outpaced the recipients after funding.

In physics funding clearly affected Ph.D. production. This can be seen both in Figure 8-3 and in the separate breakdowns for the public and private sectors. The effect here is more dramatic than in either of the other science fields. However, as in those fields, doctorate production by both the USD and medium control schools falls well below the number produced by the leading institutions. For example, the peak year in doctorate production for the USD group in physics was 1971 in which the average USD department produced 15.5 doctorates. In that same year the medium controls produced 12.8 doctorates; the high controls, 37.0!

In chemistry the medium controls exhibited higher rates than the recipient institutions before, during, and after the funding. This was true in both the private and public sectors. Note also in chemistry that the gap between the high controls, which as usual produced the most doctorates, and the other two groups is smaller than in the fields of mathematics and physics.

There are some intriguing results in the field of history. Prior to Science Development funding the USD group had been producing more doctorates per year than the medium controls in history. After funding this trend continued and the gap widened in both the public and private sectors—a finding difficult to interpret. It could represent a spillover effect of Science Development funds. Further exploration of this trend in history showed that it was sharpest in those institutions that were characterized by relatively low levels of federal science support as contrasted with those receiving substantial federal science support.

Examination of science doctorate production in those schools with substantial total federal science support as contrasted with those receiving moderate support revealed few differences in math and chemistry. In physics, the effects noted above were seen dramatically in the schools with low support, but were not seen in those schools characterized by high federal support. Thus, as might be expected, Science Development funds had their greatest impact on those schools in which they represented a greater share of the budget.

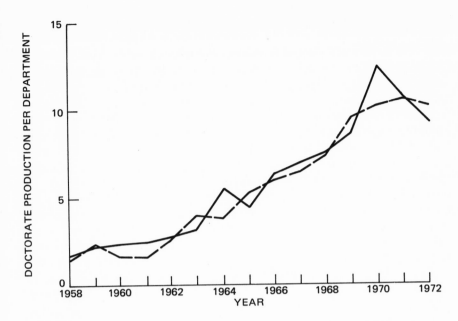

FIGURE 8-2 Doctorate production in science development and control institutions: mathematics.

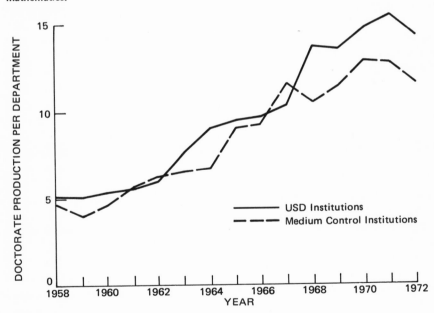

FIGURE 8-3 Doctorate production in science development and control institutions: physics.

143

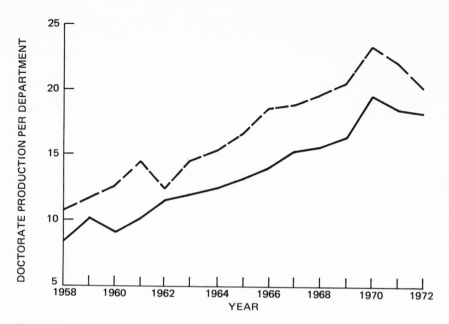

FIGURE 8-4 Doctorate production in science development and control institutions: chemistry.

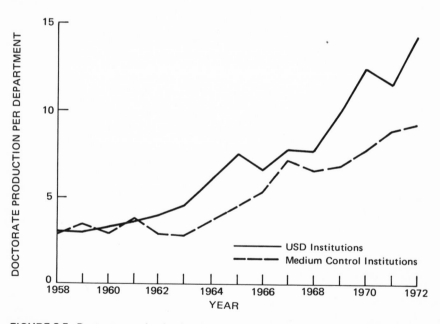

FIGURE 8-5 Doctorate production in science development and control institutions: history.

144

As before, these analyses of basic trends were supplemented with a multivariate analysis to isolate the unique effects of Science Development funds. A number of dimensions representing prefunding departmental factors likely to affect subsequent doctoral production were used as the independent variables in a series of multiple regression equations:

1. Total departmental graduate enrollment;
2. Departmental faculty size;
3. Departmental publication rate;
4. Total federal science support for the institution.

The variables were created in the same manner described in previous chapters; in most cases this meant computing the average of the values for the years 1959–1961.

These independent variables were systematically regressed on doctorate production for each year from 1965 through 1972. In Table 8-5 the results from these regressions are presented as are the partial correlations of the dummy variable, indicating whether a department got a grant, with the criterion and the partial correlation of total departmental funds with the criterion. In Figure 8-6 the mean residual scores (actual doctorate production minus predicted doctorate production) for the two key groups are plotted for the period 1965–1972. Inspection of these results indicates that, basically, these multivariate analyses substantiate the trends observed in the zero-order profiles.

COMPARISON OF Ph.D.s' FIRST JOBS

The focus of the Science Development program and of this assessment was on quality in graduate education. Though rate of Ph.D. production is an important index, it is basically quantitative. To supplement the above analyses with some that addressed the issue of quality more directly, we examined the nature of the first jobs taken by Ph.D.s from recipient and control institutions.

The unemployment of Ph.D.s has received considerable attention in the media, of course. But for virtually all of the years covered by this study, the percentage of unemployed Ph.D.s was so low that it was impossible to examine these trends meaningfully. In addition, as Niland has commented:

For most of the lower skills, the rate of unemployment serves as a reasonably accurate barometer of labor market conditions. However, for the more highly skilled the state of the market may be only weakly reflected in the employment rate. High level manpower tends to by mobile and thus has the ability, mainly by working in lesser capacities, to disguise or at least delay detection of a loosening market.[10]

[10] Niland, op. cit., p. 141.

145

TABLE 8-5 Prediction of Doctorate Production, 1965–1972

	1965	1966	1967	1968	1969	1970	1971	1972
Mathematics (N = 65)								
Multiple correlation	0.90	0.89	0.91	0.88	0.88	0.83	0.87	0.88
Regression coefficients[a]								
Faculty size	0.06	0.02	-0.04	-0.00	0.13	0.08	0.12	0.17
Publication rate	0.62	0.73	0.70	0.68	0.68	0.56	0.41	0.62
Enrollment	0.16	0.08	0.23	0.18	0.21	0.24	0.27	0.10
Science funding to university	0.15	0.12	0.08	0.08	-0.06	0.04	0.18	0.10
Partial correlations[b]								
Science development grant	-0.12	-0.07	0.04	-0.00	0.06	0.22	0.13	-0.01
All federal funds to department	-0.16	0.12	0.12	0.04	0.07	0.29	0.27	0.39
Chemistry (N = 88)								
Multiple correlation	0.91	0.90	0.90	0.89	0.85	0.90	0.88	0.87
Regression coefficients[a]								
Faculty size	0.10	0.16	0.10	0.15	0.05	0.17	0.26	0.26
Publication rate	0.41	0.38	0.43	0.24	0.36	0.14	0.26	0.10
Enrollment	0.43	0.37	0.38	0.42	0.39	0.54	0.31	0.42
Science funding to university	0.06	0.09	0.08	0.21	0.13	0.17	0.19	0.24
Partial correlations[b]								
Science development grant	-0.08	0.00	-0.09	0.01	-0.01	0.00	0.06	0.08
All federal funds to department	-0.00	0.22	0.12	0.00	0.24			

Physics (N = 65)

Multiple correlation	0.89	0.91	0.93	0.87	0.89	0.89	0.81	0.85
Regression coefficients[a]								
Faculty size	0.11	0.13	0.08	0.15	0.28	0.17	0.10	0.17
Publication rate	0.63	0.65	0.61	0.43	0.34	0.15	0.34	0.20
Enrollment	0.11	0.16	0.14	0.24	0.21	0.33	0.23	0.21
Science funding to university	0.13	0.06	0.20	0.16	0.20	0.37	0.25	0.39
Partial correlations[b]								
Science development grant	-0.02	0.06	-0.15	0.18	0.08	0.06	0.11	0.16
All federal funds to department	0.24	-0.14	0.19	0.24	0.19	0.43	0.34	0.18

History (N = 72)

Multiple correlation	0.88	0.88	0.90	0.87	0.87	0.82	0.81	0.84
Regression coefficients[a]								
Faculty size	-0.07	0.10	0.02	0.03	0.01	-0.03	0.11	0.15
Publication rate	0.58	0.60	0.67	0.36	0.50	0.42	0.19	0.18
Enrollment	0.55	0.43	0.43	0.69	0.46	0.50	0.46	0.52
Science funding to university	-0.10	-0.15	-0.13	-0.15	0.01	0.02	0.16	0.10
Partial correlations[b]								
Science development grant	0.08	0.05	0.01	0.22	-0.02	0.01	0.06	0.09

[a] Regression coefficients are standardized.
[b] Partials controlled for the three variables above.

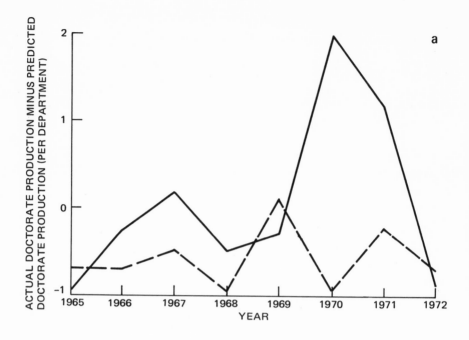

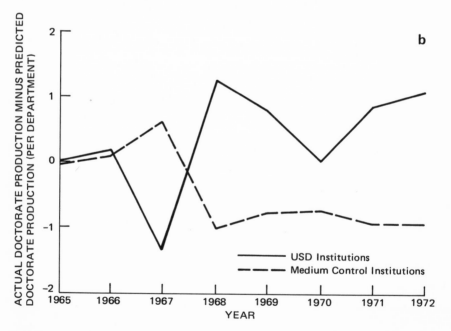

FIGURE 8-6 Residual analysis of doctorate production: (a) mathematics, (b) physics, (c) chemistry, (d) history.

148

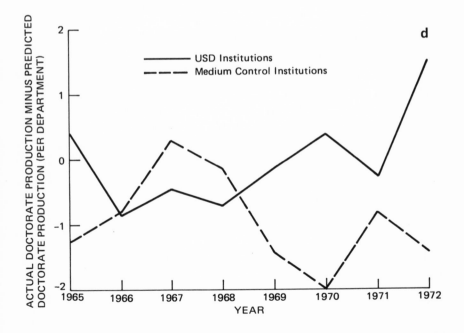

TABLE 8-6 Average Cartter Rating of Academic Departments at Which Graduates of Science Development and Control Institutions Took Their First Job, 1962–1972

	No.	1962	1963	1964	1965	1966	1967	1968	1969	1970	1971	1972
Mathematics												
USD recipients	15	0.81	1.11	1.31	1.10	1.38	1.04	1.35	—	—	0.62	0.56
DSD recipients	5	1.14	1.82	1.39	1.25	1.46	1.21	1.12	—	—	0.40	0.00
High controls	17	2.66	2.29	2.65	2.33	2.48	2.35	2.16	—	—	1.37	1.68
Medium controls	15	2.05	1.10	1.27	1.66	1.73	0.86	0.89	—	—	0.32	0.45
Low controls	16	0.56	0.76	0.42	0.42	0.82	0.77	0.47	—	—	0.28	0.53
Physics												
USD recipients	25	1.85	2.00	1.73	1.56	2.09	0.37	0.58	—	—	0.38	0.38
DSD recipients	9	2.02	1.32	0.94	1.18	0.55	0.91	0.35	—	—	0.30	0.00
High controls	14	2.56	2.73	2.95	2.70	3.01	1.70	1.84	—	—	1.05	1.30
Medium controls	18	1.20	2.17	1.51	1.42	2.28	0.80	0.35	—	—	0.69	0.41
Low controls	19	0.00	0.33	0.38	0.63	0.70	0.11	0.00	—	—	0.30	0.33
Chemistry												
USD recipients	22	0.50	1.93	1.62	1.68	2.36	0.29	0.40	—	—	0.46	0.48
DSD recipients	12	0.93	1.60	1.47	0.82	1.13	0.20	0.57	—	—	0.28	0.43
High controls	15	2.48	2.45	3.05	2.67	2.93	1.37	1.67	—	—	1.05	1.74
Medium controls	17	1.86	1.79	1.57	0.98	2.13	0.62	0.70	—	—	0.54	0.45
Low controls	24	1.34	1.11	1.05	0.90	1.04	0.27	0.20	—	—	0.13	0.00

Thus, we focused not on unemployment rates but on a comparison of the degree to which graduates of recipient and control departments were "working in lesser capacities." Those Ph.D.s who were employed after receiving their degree could have been working in either academic or non-academic jobs. Some of the characteristics associated with both types of employments are examined below.

The analyses of post-Ph.D. academic employment were conducted using national data from the Doctorate Record File of the NRC and the National Register compiled by NSF. The latter, a biannual survey conducted through the scientific professional societies, gathers information on all scientists and engineers currently working in the United States; one subgroup is scientists who have received their Ph.D. in a given year. The overall response rate is about 70 percent, though it varies from field to field. Although the survey asks about current employment only, we have assumed that this represented the first job for those who had received their Ph.D. within the previous two years. During the 15-year period covered by this study, National Register surveys including a question on current employment were conducted in 1964 and 1966. Using these surveys, we gathered data on the postdoctorate employment of graduates from the 1962, 1963, 1964, 1965, and 1966 cohorts. For each subsequent year we drew upon the Doctorate Record File. Beginning in 1967 with the unfortunate omission of 1969 and 1970, the Doctorate Record File survey instrument asked about the institution at which the Ph.D. planned to work.

In summary, data on postdoctorate academic employment were gathered for the years 1962–1968 and 1971–1972 by combined use of the National Register and the Doctorate Record File. The latter provided more complete survey information than the former.

Table 8-6 presents data on the postgraduate academic employment of Ph.D.s from recipient and control institutions for physics, chemistry, and mathematics.[11] Each entry is the average Cartter faculty quality rating of the departments *to which* graduates from that group of institutions in that year went to teach. To illustrate, in 1968, the typical graduate of a USD mathematics department took his first job at an institution where the Cartter rating of the math department was 1.35. Unfortunately, if one assumes that Ph.D.s whose graduate training was strongly affected by Science Development funding graduated in 1968 at the earliest, the only clear measure of postfunding employment are the data on 1971 and 1972.

The data for the USD and medium control groups are plotted in Figures 8-7, 8-8, and 8-9.

Some of the entries in Table 8-6 had to be based on relatively small

[11] The National Register does not provide information about Ph.D.s from the control field of history.

151

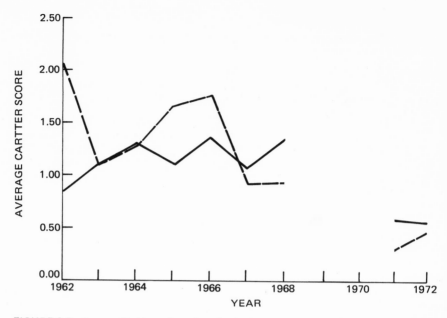

FIGURE 8-7 Average Cartter rating of academic departments at which graduates of science development and control institutions took their first job: mathematics.

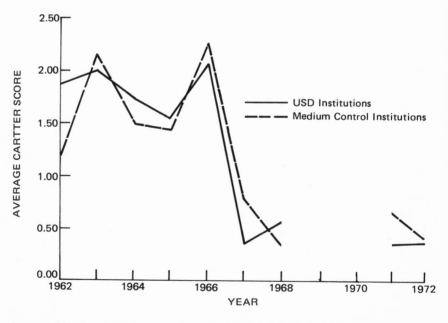

FIGURE 8-8 Average Cartter rating of academic departments at which graduates of science development and control institutions took their first job: physics.

152

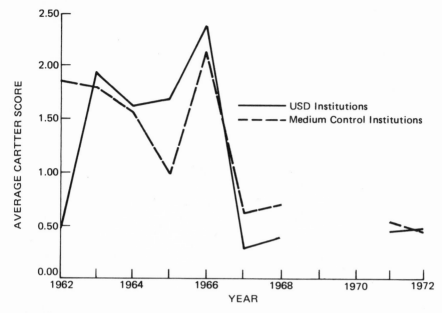

FIGURE 8-9 Average Cartter rating of academic departments at which graduates of science development and control institutions took their first job: chemistry.

samples. As an aid to the reader the sample sizes on which all Table 8-6 entries are based are given in Table 8-7.

As one might expect, Ph.D.s from all levels of institutions are going to less highly ranked institutions these days than in the past as a result of the tight job market in academia. Virtually all of the trends reported in this table are down. This is the so-called trickle effect that Niland and others have discussed.

Table 8-6 reveals that while all graduates were going to poorer jobs in the later years, this was relatively less true of Science Development graduates than of control graduates from private institutions in mathematics. Otherwise the USDs and medium controls were landing comparable jobs in the most recent years.[12]

New doctorate recipients often seek jobs outside the academic sphere; the nonacademic, industrial sector is a major employer of these scientists.

[12] A subgroup (approximately one third) from each graduating cohort took jobs at undergraduate colleges, i.e., in departments which were not rated by Cartter. In the data reported above these departments were assigned a Cartter rating of zero.

In addition, a special reanalysis of the data was conducted in which this subgroup of Ph.D.s was excluded. When only Ph.D.s who took jobs at Cartter-rated departments were studied, the result did not differ markedly from those reported above. Essentially, in all three science fields, Ph.D.s from the USD and the medium control groups were found to be taking jobs in comparably rated departments in 1971 and 1972.

TABLE 8-7   Sample Sizes on Which the Entries in Table 8-6 Are Based

	No.	1962	1963	1964	1965	1966	1967	1968	1969	1970	1971	1972
Mathematics												
USD recipients	15	12	22	40	39	26	56	39	—	—	95	26
DSD recipeints	5	3	4	5	6	2	1	14	—	—	15	8
High controls	17	42	122	158	159	69	151	110	—	—	225	119
Medium controls	15	16	29	40	33	20	48	43	—	—	77	32
Low controls	16	9	26	29	27	9	28	31	—	—	44	18
Physics												
USD recipients	25	18	51	111	88	60	51	36	—	—	61	19
DSD recipeints	9	3	11	15	12	9	10	13	—	—	23	6
High controls	14	37	108	121	149	94	42	19	—	—	50	20
Medium controls	18	8	19	51	51	49	33	15	—	—	42	15
Low controls	19	4	16	28	16	16	14	16	—	—	22	12
Chemistry												
USD recipients	22	14	56	68	51	52	32	32	—	—	52	22
DSD recipeints	12	3	18	21	16	14	11	10	—	—	28	6
High controls	15	31	83	114	104	45	61	35	—	—	56	23
Medium controls	17	15	54	69	62	47	35	25	—	—	54	15
Low controls	24	7	13	32	20	36	19	21	—	—	23	11

154

TABLE 8-8 Average Salaries Received by Graduates of Science Development and Control Institutions in Their First Nonacademic Job, 1958-1970

	No.	1958	1959	1960	1961	1962	1963	1964	1965	1966	1967	1968	1969	1970
Physics														
USD recipients	25	11,231	10,222	10,618	11,282	11,204	12,407	12,768	11,781	13,279	14,231	15,160	15,582	14,889
High controls	14	10,707	10,160	10,586	10,770	10,795	11,125	11,594	12,576	13,312	13,646	15,282	14,965	15,015
Medium controls	18	11,000	11,533	10,488	12,069	11,500	12,510	13,220	13,107	14,173	14,207	16,024	15,353	14,678
Low controls	19	11,000	11,700	10,308	12,375	11,122	11,971	11,021	12,843	12,170	14,479	15,075	15,400	16,322
Chemistry														
USD recipients	22	9,885	9,262	9,086	10,486	10,564	11,551	11,315	12,320	12,699	13,557	14,237	14,070	14,568
DSD recipients	12	9,368	8,786	10,263	10,053	10,428	10,492	11,595	11,632	12,233	13,046	14,167	14,592	14,429
High controls	15	9,438	8,953	9,714	10,100	10,305	10,943	11,361	11,989	12,358	13,417	13,478	14,762	14,450
Medium controls	17	9,784	10,031	9,339	10,553	11,093	11,295	11,611	12,170	12,716	13,220	13,320	14,862	14,182
Low controls	24	9,410	9,484	9,174	10,381	10,317	11,535	11,148	11,673	12,080	13,826	14,566	14,321	14,236

155

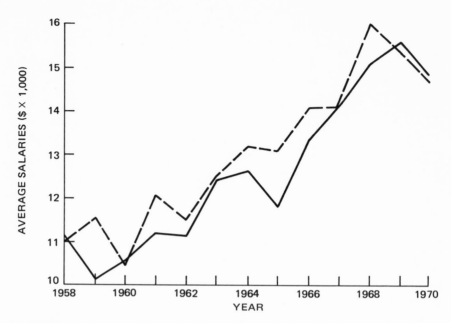

FIGURE 8-10 Average salaries received by graduates of science development and control institutions in their first nonacademic job: physics.

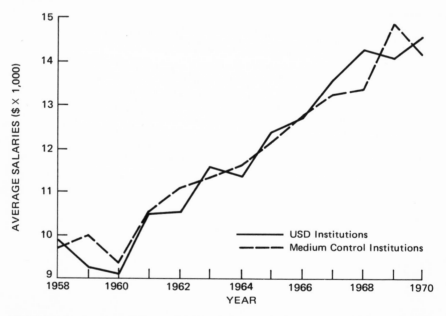

FIGURE 8-11 Average salaries received by graduates of science development and control institutions in their first nonacademic job: chemistry.

TABLE 8-9 Sample Sizes on Which the Entries in Table 8-8 are Based

	No.	1958	1959	1960	1961	1962	1963	1964	1965	1966	1967	1968	1969	1970
Physics														
USD recipients	25	52	36	34	39	47	57	44	57	38	48	50	72	19
High controls	14	58	81	70	61	88	93	72	70	58	81	39	63	26
Medium controls	18	25	30	43	29	25	48	20	44	22	43	34	45	18
Low controls	19	6	10	13	16	18	21	14	14	10	24	12	19	9
Chemistry														
USD recipients	22	78	65	58	70	72	90	62	71	91	97	63	94	38
DSD recipients	12	19	14	19	19	18	24	19	28	24	26	21	37	17
High controls	15	73	64	64	80	75	81	79	91	60	81	60	84	28
Medium controls	17	51	65	62	38	43	62	62	90	55	93	61	81	22
Low controls	24	39	31	23	21	29	20	25	30	35	38	29	43	14

Thus, we also analyzed the first jobs of those Ph.D.s from experimental and control institutions who did not enter college and university jobs. This analysis drew exclusively upon the National Register, which, in every survey conducted during the time frame under consideration, had asked the respondent about his current salary. Salary was the one indicator of the status of an industrial job that was available for this research.

Table 8-8 shows the mean salaries of Ph.D.s from each group of institutions for the years 1958 through 1970 for physics and chemistry. In Figures 8-10 and 8-11, the means for the USD and medium control groups are plotted for each of the two fields. In Table 8-9 the corresponding sample sizes are given. (The samples for mathematics and for the DSDs in physics were so sparse that the data had to be omitted.)

Some obvious general conclusions can be drawn. Salaries rose at a fairly steady rate over the years, reflecting inflation. The salaries of graduates from Science Development institutions and from control institutions climbed at about the same rate. In general, Science Development funds did not seem to have a major effect on this trend, nor did the graduates from the recipient institutions suffer dramatically in comparison with the controls. In short, the salaries achieved by Ph.D.s from the two groups tended to be about the same at all time points.[13]

[13] A close inspection of Table 8-8 reveals very few differences in salary levels, even between the high and the low controls. Thus, although tracing salary data seemed a valuable exercise (particularly since it was the sole index available of the status of an industrial job), this parameter cannot be considered a measure of graduate department quality. This, in itself, is an intriguing finding.

9 Summary

This technical report has presented in detail the findings from an evaluative study of the National Science Foundation's Science Development program. The study was requested by the NSF Evaluation Unit in 1971, the same year in which the funding program ended.

The Science Development program (described in detail in Chapter 2) was a pioneering experiment in institutional funding initiated in 1965 with the goal of dramatically increasing the number of "centers of excellence" in graduate science education. In the early 1960s criticism had been directed against the concentration of federal funds and national science talent in a few universities, disproportionately clustered in the Northeast. The major objective of Science Development was to stimulate high-level science activity at second-tier institutions dispersed geographically throughout the nation.

There were three subprograms under Science Development. By far the largest and most important was University Science Development (USD), under which funds totaling $177 million were given to 31 universities that seemed to have potential for developing superior science capabilities. Under USD, several science departments—typically four or five—in each university were funded over a period of five to seven years. The second subprogram, Departmental Science Development (DSD), awarded 73 grants to single departments considered to have the potential for high quality but located in universities that generally were too weak to qualify for the larger USD subprogram. Finally, 11 Special Science Development (SSD) grants were given to universities that fell between the two poles represented by USD and DSD.

159

The basic purpose of this evaluation study was to examine the impact of Science Development funding on the recipient departments and institutions. A second objective was to assess the relative efficacy of the subprograms. In addition to these fundamental issues, the study was concerned with a number of related questions: Were nonfunded departments in funded universities affected? What happened in the funded universities when these massive government grants ended? The methodology was developed to address these substantive concerns, as well as to satisfy the technical demands of effective assessment.

METHODOLOGY

Answering the basic questions required tackling the thorny issue of the meaning of "quality" science education in American graduate schools. An early decision was made to use multiple indicators or criteria of quality. We hope that this research has contributed toward a definition of quality graduate education in terms that can be operationalized for scientific research.

The methodology combined two approaches: (1) case studies, carried out by site visits at selected institutions, and (2) multivariate analysis of quantitative data on institutions.

The site visits were conducted at 16 recipient institutions and five nonfunded (control) institutions, which were studied for purposes of comparison. Of the recipient institutions, nine had been awarded USD grants, six had received one or more DSD grants, and one had been awarded an SSD grant. For the smaller DSD recipients, the site-visit teams included a senior member of the project staff (typically the project director) and a scientist who had been on the original NSF team that reviewed the proposal submitted by the university. For the USD and SSD recipients, the teams were larger; in addition to a senior member of the project staff, they included one or two scientists who had visited the university previously, skilled and experienced academic administrators, and researchers specializing in higher education assessment. Where possible, members of the Study Advisory Panel and the National Board on Graduate Education joined the team.

A wide range of institutions was visited: public and private; funded and nonfunded; those where the grants were thought to be successful and those where they were thought to have failed. However, in light of the NSF emphasis on regional dispersion of the funds, we deliberately attempted to visit schools all over the country. Table 3-1 summarizes the distribution of site-visit institutions with respect to control (public or private), region, and type of grant.

At each institution, members of the site team met with the chief administrator, the institutional representative for the Science Development grant, provosts, deans, and other high officials. In addition, they conducted in-depth visits to both funded and nonfunded departments, interviewing department chairmen, faculty members, and graduate students and examining equipment and facilities acquired under Science Development support.

For the quantitative analyses, both longitudinal data and complex statistical techniques were required to isolate the unique effects of Science Development. Wherever possible, the information gathered for this study covered the 15 years from 1958 through 1972. Thus, by going back for several years prior to the launching of Science Development (1965), we were able to identify trends already under way at the institutions.

To assess the impact of Science Development, it was necessary to compare trends in funded institutions with trends in nonfunded (control) institutions. So that these comparisons would be as thorough and as meaningful as possible, we selected for the control group not just a few institutions but every major doctorate-producing institution in the nation. Thus, the sample comprised all universities rated by Roose and Andersen in their 1969 evaluation of graduate education in the United States. This procedure enabled us to compare Science Development institutions with nonfunded institutions of roughly similar initial quality (the "medium controls"), with universities considered already outstanding in science (the "high controls"), and with institutions whose science capabilities were considered generally unpromising (the "low controls").

As indicated above, multiple criteria were used to operationalize the concept of science quality. These criteria were faculty size and publication rates, graduate student enrollment size, test scores and baccalaureate origins of graduate students, Ph.D. production, and characteristics of institutions at which Ph.D.s took their first jobs.

SITE VISITS

The case studies that emerged from the site visits yielded a number of general observations about the effects—both good and bad—of Science Development.

Clearly, Science Development funds were responsible for many desirable changes; some universities made a quantum leap forward with the aid of these funds. Concrete evidence of the program's positive impact include brilliant new faculty members acquired, graduate enrollments increased, buildings constructed, a telescope built, exciting interdisciplinary institutes formed, etc. Basically, Science Development funds served as a catalyst, allowing the recipient universities to accelerate the development of their science capabilities. While it would not be accurate to say that the

161

program created "centers of excellence" in the sense that all the funded institutions are now the academic peers of Berkeley and Cal Tech, the improvement was, in most cases, notable.

The program's most obvious negative effect was tied to the erratic pattern of overall federal support for graduate education. In most schools, the support from Science Development was ending at the same time that the widely publicized financial crunch in higher education hit. Many institutions had to struggle in order to fulfill their commitment to maintain the improvements initiated under Science Development. All too often, other departments in the institution suffered as a result of this emphasis on the sciences. In short, Science Development funds had the effect of distorting the overall balance at some institutions.

Perhaps the key factor that distinguished successful grants from those that were less so was the strength of an institution's central administration, especially its president or chancellor. This person's continuity in office was particularly important. Grants tended to be regarded as most successful at universities that had a strong and dynamic leader who was in office before, during, and after the grant. An equally important factor—and one closely associated with a strong central administration—was the existence of a detailed development plan. Such plans often served as the foundation for a Science Development proposal that then was likely to contribute to balanced overall growth.

In fact, one of the secondary benefits of Science Development was that it forced those universities that had previously failed to plan for science to develop such plans. Thus, even those institutions whose requests for funding were rejected by the Foundation may have reaped some advantage from the organized thought required to develop a proposal.

Science Development funds had a number of indirect effects on nonfunded departments at recipient institutions. For instance, the development of support facilities like a computer center may have benefited a spectrum of departments. As another example, a particular department at an institution that received a USD grant may have been judged too weak to merit funding; in some cases, the institution itself then made special efforts to develop this weak department at the same time that USD funding was building up the other science areas.

The site-visit teams heard numerous testimonials to the flexibility of those NSF officials who had administered the program and worked with the institutions. A retrospective comparison of funded vs. nonfunded institutions, and of funded vs. nonfunded departments in the same institution, attested to the validity of NSF's judgment in selecting or rejecting applicants. In retrospect, however, it seems clear that the Foundation should have required more in the way of evaluation and documentation from the institutions as a condition of receiving these massive grants.

162

QUANTITATIVE ANALYSIS

The use of quantitative analyses permitted us to pinpoint the unique effects of Science Development funding on the criteria of excellence listed above. All analyses were repeated in each of the three primary science fields funded by the program (mathematics, physics, and chemistry) and in a control field, history.

Faculty Size

Since a large segment of a typical Science Development award was earmarked for "personnel" and since most scientists believe that the way to develop a department is to hire excellent people, we first questioned whether changes in departmental faculty sizes resulted from the funding. The results of this analysis were clear-cut and dramatic. There is no question that the NSF funds enabled the recipient departments to increase their faculties. This growth was evident in the three science fields but not in history. For physics and chemistry, the growth in faculty size was limited to the public sector; in the private sector the recipient institutions had larger faculties than the controls prior to funding, a difference that persisted through 1972.

A central issue surrounding Science Development was whether these increases in the faculty sizes of funded departments were made at the expense of nonfunded departments, particularly those in the leading institutions. Some critics of the program charged that it represented no net gain for the nation but merely enabled the recipient institutions to "steal" outstanding scientists from the "best" research universities. This assertion was subjected to an empirical test in a special analysis of faculty mobility in the field of physics (see Chapter 5). The analysis revealed that grants allowed the recipient institutions to maintain the growth rate established prior to funding, whereas the growth rate of the medium controls slowed down considerably during the funding period. The sources of senior faculty for the physics recipients under funding did not differ markedly from that before funding. Moreover, it is clear that any defections by senior faculty from leading institutions to the USD recipients were trivial before, during, and after funding.

Faculty Productivity

Next, we looked at scholarly productivity, as measured by rate of publication in key journals. To select the leading journals in physics, chemistry, and mathematics, we ranked-ordered all journals in each field on the basis of an impact factor: i.e., the ratio of citations to a given journal (in other journals) divided by the number of source articles in that journal. (A slightly different, but analogous, procedure was necessary for the control field of history.) The journal at the top of the list, then, was the one in which an article would have the greatest impact in that other scientists would cite it frequently in their work. During the ranking process, various technical adjustments were made for such factors as the representation of American authors in English-language journals published in other countries. The list for each field was limited to about 20 leading journals, but these journals accounted for a majority of the citations in that field. In physics, for example, the list of 20 represented over 75 percent of all citations.

Next, the rate of publication in these journals by faculty in funded and in control institutions was plotted between 1958 and 1972. In addition, to isolate the unique effects of Science Development, we carried out a multivariate analysis, in which residual scores were derived.

National Science Foundation funding had a positive impact on departmental productivity in each of the three science fields. In chemistry this effect was revealed only through the multivariate analysis, but in math and physics it was clear from the zero-order analysis. The increase in departmental publication rates at funded institutions was greatest in mathematics, definite in physics, and slight in chemistry. The trend in mathematics was found in both the public and private sectors.

The Science Development program had less impact on per person productivity. Although the data for mathematics seemed to indicate an increase in the publication rates of individual faculty members, the residual analysis raises a question as to whether this increase was attributable to Science Development funding or was an artifact of other factors. The multivariate analysis revealed a possible impact on the publication rates of individual chemists. No such effects were found for either physics or the control field of history.

In short, recipient science departments clearly improved their publication rates with the aid of Science Development funding. But this improvement was a departmental change, probably resulting in large part simply from the increase in faculty size. The effects on per person productivity were minimal.

Graduate Students: Enrollments and Quality

Next, the impact of Science Development funding on enrollments, a quantitative measure, and quality, defined in terms of the GRE test scores and baccalaureate origins of entering graduate students, was assessed. The receipt of a Science Development grant had very little effect either on total graduate enrollments or on first-year, full-time graduate enrollments. The one exception was found among public recipient institutions,

164

where graduate enrollments in mathematics increased, apparently as a result of the funding.

A special retrieval effort was conducted to gather information on the GRE scores of students entering a funded department, chemistry, and the control department of history in a prefunding and a postfunding year. Comparison of the changes revealed that the former group improved their relative standing significantly during this time period. In short, there seemed to be an effect of Science Development funding upon the GRE scores of students entering recipient chemistry departments. However, findings from the control field of history suggested that the changes on the quantitative component of the test might be the result of factors other than NSF funding.

As another measure of the quality of graduate students, we looked at the baccalaureate origins of students entering funded and control graduate departments. Specifically, we wanted to see if the graduate students attracted to the recipient departments after funding tended to come from more highly selective undergraduate institutions. No such trend was found.

Doctorate Production

The crisis facing graduate education today derives in part from the highly publicized surplus of Ph.D.s in some fields, a surplus indicated by the relatively high unemployment rates of this select group. Some critics have charged that the Science Development program contributed to this problem by accelerating the production of Ph.D.s. A special set of analyses was devoted to examining the effects of Science Development funding on Ph.D. production and to tracing the subsequent employment of Ph.D.s from recipient and control institutions.

Data from the Doctorate Record File of the National Research Council allowed us to plot Ph.D. production in each of the three science fields and in history for the period 1958–1972. In mathematics, the data indicated that Science Development funds increased the production of doctorates in the public sector but not in the private sector. National Science Foundation funding had its most dramatic effect on Ph.D. production in physics, where it was apparent in both the public and the private sectors. In chemistry, no relationship was found between funding and the production of Ph.D.s. It should be noted that even in mathematics and physics, the number of Ph.D.s from both the USD and the medium control schools fell well below the number from the leading institutions. For example, in 1971—the peak year for the USD group in physics—the average recipient department produced 15.5 doctorates, the medium controls produced 12.8 doctorates, but the high controls produced 37.0!

The rate of Ph.D. production, though important, is a quantitative

165

measure. To get at the issue of *quality* more directly, the nature of the first jobs taken by Ph.D.s from recipient and control institutions were reviewed; separate analyses for those entering academia and those taking non-academic jobs were performed.

For the former, we examined the [Cartter] faculty quality rating given to the department at which graduates of funded and of control institutions took their first job. As one might expect, in view of the tight job market in academia, Ph.D.s from all groups of institutions are going into more poorly ranked institutions these days than in the past. But this was less true for Science Development Ph.D.s than for control Ph.D.s from private institutions in the field of mathematics. Otherwise, Ph.D.s from funded and from control institutions fared about the same in the postfunding years.

Salary was the one indicator of the status of a nonacademic job that was available for this research. Analysis revealed that the starting salaries of graduates from Science Development schools and from control schools rose at about the same rate.

CONCLUSIONS

Most evaluation studies of federal funding programs are hard pressed to find any discernible impact. It is clear at the conclusion of this study that the NSF Science Development program was a powerful enough force in graduate education that several years after its demise, its impact can be seen in a variety of ways. On the face of it, some of these impacts were positive, some negative. The goal of this study has been to determine objectively whether or not effects occurred. The interpretation of their value is a philosophical decision that we leave to the reader.

Appendix A
Composition of Samples

MATHEMATICS

USD Recipients

Arizona
Brooklyn
Polytechnic Institute
Carnegie-Mellon
Colorado
Florida
Louisiana State
Maryland
Michigan State
Notre Dame
Oregon
Rice
Rutgers
Tulane
USC
Virginia

DSD (and Special) Recipients

Claremont
Denver
Kentucky
New Mexico State
RPI

High Controls

Brandeis
Brown
California, Berkeley
California Institute of
    Technology
Chicago
Columbia
Cornell
Harvard
Illinois
Michigan
Minnesota
MIT
Princeton
Stanford
UCLA
Wisconsin
Yale

Medium Controls

Illinois Institute of
    Technology
Iowa State (Ames)
Johns Hopkins
Kansas
Lehigh

Missouri
Northwestern
Ohio State
Oklahoma
Oregon State
Penn State
Pennsylvania
Syracuse
Wayne State
Yeshiva

Low Controls

Alabama
American
Boston University
Catholic
Cincinnati
George Peabody
George Washington
Nebraska
Oklahoma State
St. Louis
SUNY, Buffalo
Tennessee
Texas A&M
Utah
VPI
Washington State

167

PHYSICS

USD Receipients

Arizona
Brooklyn Polytechnic Institute
Carnegie-Mellon
Case Western Reserve
Colorado
Duke
Florida
Florida State
Indiana
Louisiana State
Maryland
Michigan State
New York University
North Carolina
Notre Dame
Oregon
Pittsburgh
Purdue
Rutgers
Texas
USC
Vanderbilt
Virginia
Washington (Seattle)
Washington (St. Louis)

DSD (and Special) Recipients

Brandeis
Delaware
Nebraska
Ohio University
Stevens Institute
Tennessee
Utah
Washington State
Yeshiva

High Controls

California, Berkeley
California Institute of
    Technology
Chicago
Columbia
Cornell
Harvard
Illinois
Michigan
MIT
Pennsylvania
Princeton
Stanford
Wisconsin
Yale

Medium Controls

Boston University
Brown
Catholic
Illinois Institute of
    Technology
Iowa State (Ames)
Johns Hopkins
Kansas
Lehigh
Minnesota
Northwestern
Ohio State
Oregon State
Penn. State
RPI
Syracuse
Texas A&M
Tufts
UCLA
Wayne State

Low Controls

Alabama
Bryn Mawr
Cincinnati
Connecticut
Emory
Fordham
Georgetown
George Washington
Georgia Tech
Kansas State
Kentucky
Missouri
New Mexico
Oklahoma
St. Louis
SUNY, Buffalo
Temple
VPI
West Virginia

CHEMISTRY

USD Recipients

Arizona
Brooklyn Polytechnic Institute
Carnegie-Mellon
Case Western Reserve
Colorado
Duke
Florida
Florida State
Indiana
Louisiana State
Maryland
Michigan State
North Carolina
Notre Dame
Oregon
Pittsburgh
Rochester
Texas
USC
Vanderbilt
Virginia
Washington (St. Louis)

DSD (and Special) Recipients

Brandeis
Bryn Mawr
Emory
Hawaii
Nebraska
Oregon State
RPI
South Carolina
Texas A&M
Utah
Washington State
Wayne State

High Controls

California, Berkeley
California Institute of
    Technology

168

Chicago
Columbia
Cornell
Harvard
Illinois
Minnesota
MIT
Northwestern
Princeton
Stanford
UCLA
Wisconsin
Yale

Medium Controls

Brown
California, Davis
Cincinnati
Delaware
Georgia Tech
Illinois Institute of
  Technology
Iowa State (Ames)
Johns Hopkins
Kansas
Kansas State
Massachusetts
Michigan
Ohio State
Penn State
Pennsylvania
SUNY, Buffalo
Tennessee

Low Controls

Alabama
Arkansas
Boston University
Catholic
Clark
Connecticut
Fordham
Georgetown
George Washington
Houston
Kentucky
Lehigh
Loyola (Chicago)

Missouri
New Mexico
Oklahoma
Oklahoma State
St. Louis
Syracuse
Temple
Tufts
VPI
West Virginia
Wyoming

HISTORY

USD Recipients

Case Western Reserve
Colorado
Duke
Florida
Indiana
Iowa (Iowa City)
Louisiana State
Maryland
Michigan State
New York University
North Carolina
Notre Dame
Oregon
Pittsburgh
Rice
Rochester
Rutgers
Texas
Tulane
USC
Vanderbilt
Virginia
Washington (Seattle)
Washington (St. Louis)

High Controls

California, Berkeley
Chicago
Columbia
Cornell
Harvard
Johns Hopkins

Michigan
Northwestern
Pennsylvania
Princeton
Stanford
UCLA
Wisconsin
Yale

Medium Controls

Brandeis
Brown
Claremont
Clark
Emory
Gerogetown
George Washington
Illinois
Kansas
Kentucky
Minnesota
Missouri
Nebraska
Ohio State
Oklahoma
Penn State
Syracuse
Wayne State

Low Controls

Alabama
American
Arkansas
Boston University
Catholic
Cincinnati
Fordham
George Peabody
Lehigh
Loyola (Chicago)
New Mexico
North Dakota
St. Johns (N.Y.)
St. Louis
SUNY, Buffalo
Utah
Washington State
West Virginia

SAMPLE GROUPS BASED ON THE COMBINED SCIENCE RATING

USD Recipients

Arizona
Brooklyn Polytechnic Institute
Carnegie-Mellon
Case Western Reserve
Colorado
Duke
Florida
Florida State
Indiana
Iowa (Iowa City)
Louisiana State
Maryland
Michigan State
New York University
North Carolina State
North Carolina
Notre Dame
Oregon
Pittsburgh
Purdue
Rice
Rochester
Rutgers
Texas
Tulane
USC
Vanderbilt
Virginia
Washington (Seattle)
Washington (St. Louis)

High Controls

California, Berkeley
California Institute of Technology

Chicago
Columbia
Cornell
Harvard
Illinois
Michigan
Minnesota
MIT
Princeton
Stanford
UCLA
Wisconsin
Yale

Medium Controls

Brandeis
Brown
Illinois Institute of Technology
Iowa State (Ames)
Johns Hopkins
Kansas
Nebraska
Northwestern
Ohio State
Oregon State
Penn State
Pennsylvania
RPI
Syracuse
Tennessee
Utah
Washington State
Wayne State

Low Controls

Alabama
American
Arkansas
Boston University
Bryn Mawr
California, Davis
Catholic
Cincinnati
Clark
Connecticut
Delaware
Fordham
Emory
George Peabody
Georgetown
George Washington
Georgia Tech
Houston
Kansas State
Kentucky
Lehigh
Loyola (Chicago)
Massachusetts
Missouri
New Mexico
Oklahoma
Oklahoma State
St. Louis
SUNY, Buffalo
Temple
Texas A&M
Tufts
VPI
West Virginia
Wyoming
Yeshiva

Appendix B
Selection of Key Journals

To develop the criteria for selecting journals, we drew on an ISI analysis of their 1969 data, in which the leading 1,000 journals in science had been rank-ordered both by number of publications and by number of citations. A third ranking, which took into consideration an "impact factor," most closely met the needs of this study. The impact factor was the ratio of citations to source articles; thus, journals ranking high on this list were those whose articles were most frequently cited, indicating that the impact of an article in that journal would be maximal. Between acquisition of the ISI list and the final selection of journals for this study, however, we had to make a number of more fine-tuned decisions.

The analyses reported in Chapter 6 cover four fields: physics, mathematics, chemistry, and history. Since the control field of history was not covered by the ISI data bank, journals in that field were selected by special methods parallel to those used in the other three fields.

First, all journals in a given field were selected from the list of 1,000: In mathematics there were 33; in physics, 66; and in chemistry, 69. Then the journals for a given field—say, mathematics—were rank-ordered by impact factor. Each journal was examined carefully for possible idiosyncrasies or problems.

The major technical problem in developing the list for each field was the presence of foreign journals. For a variety of reasons, we decided to exclude journals that were not published in the English language. Those foreign journals in which the work of American authors appear to any substantial extent tend to be English-language periodicals published in one

TABLE B-1 Journals Selected in Mathematics

Title	Impact Factor	No. 1969 Citations to 1967–1968 Articles	Source Articles (1967–1968)	Total No. 1969 Citations (All Years)
1. Annals of Mathematics	2.216	184	83	702
2. Communications on Pure and Applied Mathematics	1.935	120	62	242
3. Indiana University, Mathematics Journal	1.109	160	157	162
4. Transactions of the American Mathematical Society	0.993	300	302	709
5. Bulletin of the American Mathematical Society	0.847	356	420	347
6. Pacific Journal of Mathematics	0.759	332	437	368
7. Michigan Mathematics Journal	0.750	84	112	100
8. American Journal of Mathematics	0.607	68	112	292
9. Archive for Rational Mechanics and Analysis	0.580[a]	126[a]	137[a]	158[a]
10. Duke Mathematical Journal	0.561	100	178	240
11. Annals of Mathematical Statistics	0.511	436	853	594
12. Technometrics	0.504	124	246	135
13. National Bureau of Standards, Journal of Research (Series B)	0.472	96	203	487
14. Journal of Mathematical Analysis and Applications	0.440[a]	172[a]	289[a]	135[a]
15. Proceedings of the American Mathematical Society	0.439	256	583	436
16. Illinois Journal of Mathematics	0.437	56	128	114
17. Mathematics of Computation	0.353	104	294	95
18. Biometrika	0.342[a]	59[a]	80[a]	138[a]
19. American Statistical Association, Journal	0.332	164	493	219
20. Applied Scientific Research	0.326[a]	32[a]	39[a]	48[a]
TOTAL: journals 1–20		3,329	5,208	5,721
TOTAL: all mathematics journals		4,687	10,662	6,880
Percentage of totals covered by journals 1–20		71.0	48.8	83.2

[a] Figures adjusted for percentage of American authors. See text.

of three countries: Canada, Great Britain, and Holland. Journals published in other countries (whether in the English language or not) were also eliminated.

The impact of an eligible foreign journal was measured in terms of the American influence reflected in that journal. That is, a count was made of the proportion of articles authored by American scientists as opposed to, say, British or Canadian scientists. This proportion was then used to adjust the other figures in the selection process such as the impact factor. To illustrate, the British journal, *Advances in Physics,* has a total impact factor of 3.837 but the proportion of American scientists publishing in that journal is 13 percent. Thus, the adjusted impact factor for that journal was 0.512. Similarly, the counts of the number of citations to that journal and of the number of source articles in it were adjusted by this proportion.

As a result of this method, the 20 physics journals selected represent, in sequential order, the 20 journal outlets in which scholarly articles written by American physicists have the greatest impact.

An additional problem existed in that neither the academic world nor the world of scholarly publication is divided into neatly defined fields. Many journals deal with more than one field. Our options here were (1) to drop the multifield journal entirely, (2) to include it in both fields, assigning the same impact factor to each, or (3) to include it in both fields, assigning a different impact factor in each.

Were the first option adopted, much significant information would be lost. There appears to be no valid basis on which to make the distinctions necessary for the last option. Therefore, we decided to include multifield journals, assigning an equal impact factor for both fields involved.

Some additional criteria were applied: Abstracts and bibliographic journals were excluded, as were journals that began publication after December 31, 1962, though the latter group was included in the counts of total citations and total source articles. The few journals that do not list the corporate addresses of authors were, of necessity, excluded.

Tables B-1, B-2 and B-3 list, in order of their impact, the journals selected for the fields of mathematics, physics, and chemistry, respectively. Each table includes the journal title, the impact factor, the citation count (i.e., all 1969 citations to the journal for articles published in 1967 and 1968), the number of source articles (i.e., all source articles published in the journal in 1967 and 1968), and the total citation count for that journal in 1969[1] (i.e., all citations to the journal in 1969 for articles published in any year). As indicated above, figures for foreign journals have been adjusted to reflect the representation of American authors. In addition, the total

---

[1] In fact, ISI computed these figures by multiplying the counts for the last quarter of 1969 by four.

TABLE B-2   Journals Selected in Physics

Title	Impact Factor	No. 1969 Citations to 1967–1968 Articles	Source Articles (1967–1968)	Total No. 1969 Citations (All Years)
1. *Solid State Physics*	16.285	228	14	384
2. *Annual Review of Nuclear Science*	5.629	152	27	174
3. *Physical Review Letters*	5.114	11,380	2,225	6,581
4. *Astrophysical Journal*	4.972	5,440	1,094	4,271
5. *Review of Modern Physics*	4.508	816	181	1,364
6. *Applied Physics Letters*	3.688	2,556	693	1,337
7. *Physical Review*	3.679	20,740	5,637	20,674
8. *Journal of Geophysical Research*	3.665	5,312	1,449	3,571
9. *Inorganic Chemistry*	3.296	3,976	1,206	2,620
10. *Annals of Physics*	3.188	692	217	1,113
11. *Journal of Chemical Physics*	3.180	11,696	3,677	13,690
12. *Journal of Marine Research*	2.566	136	53	193
13. *Bulletin of the Seismological Society of America*	2.039	416	204	344
14. *Journal of the Atmospheric Sciences*	2.016	500	248	485
15. *Journal of Applied Physics*	1.936	5,124	2,646	5,299
16. *Communications on Pure and Applied Mathematics*	1.935	120	62	242
17. *Physics of Fluids*	1.581	1,548	979	1,304
18. *Space Science Review*	1.513[a]	104[a]	42[a]	83[a]
19. *Proceedings of the Institute of Electrical and Electronic Engineers*	1.372	1,856	1,352	1,610
20. *Planetary and Space Science*	1.265[a]	410[a]	149[a]	233[a]
TOTAL; journals 1–20		73,202	22,155	65,572
TOTAL; all physics journals		93,303	51,886	85,693
Percentage of totals covered by journals 1–20		78.5	42.7	76.5

[a] Figures adjusted for percentage of American authors. See text.

174

TABLE B-3 Journals Selected in Chemistry

Title	Impact Factor	No. 1969 Citations to 1967–1968 Articles	Source Articles (1967–1968)	Total No. 1969 Citations (All Years)
1. *Chemical Review*	8.680	408	47	1,003
2. *Journal of the American Chemical Society*	5.859	22,156	3,781	26,323
3. *Annual Review of Physical Chemistry*	3.555	128	36	113
4. *Inorganic Chemistry*	3.296	3,976	1,206	2,620
5. *Journal of Chemical Physics*	3.180	11,696	3,677	13,690
6. *Journal of Physical Chemistry*	2.429	4,516	1,859	4,703
7. *Journal of Organic Chemistry*	2.407	5,756	2,391	5,401
8. *Analytical Biochemistry*	2.059[a]	1,254[a]	457[a]	1,139[a]
9. *Quarterly Reviews*	1.749[a]	82[a]	9[a]	89[a]
10. *Journal of Agriculture and Food Chemistry*	1.665	728	437	512
11. *Analytical Chemistry*	1.661	2,424	1,459	4,259
12. *American Institute of Chemical Engineers, Chemical Engineering Journal*	1.559	652	418	585
13. *Journal of Applied Polymer Science*	1.395	624	447	585
14. *Photochemistry and Photobiology*	1.314[a]	305[a]	150[a]	343[a]
15. *Cereal Chemistry*	1.210	184	152	292
16. *Industrial Engineering Chemistry*	1.123	928	826	1,658
17. *Advances in Chemistry Series*	1.112	652	586	416
18. *Journal of Polymer Science*	1.039	1,912	1,839	2,914
19. *Journal of the Physics and Chemistry of Solids*	1.037[a]	786[a]	379[a]	715[a]
20. *Journal of Quantitative Spectroscopy and Radiative Transfer*	0.993[a]	249[a]	182[a]	171[a]
TOTAL journals 1–20		59,416	20,338	67,553

[a] Figures adjusted for percentage of American authors. See text.

numbers of citations to, and source articles from, the 20 selected journals combined, all journals in the field, and the proportion of the latter constituted by the former are summarized at the bottom of each table.[2]

Because history was not covered by ISI, it posed a special problem. An examination of the literature in history and consultation with historians revealed that the American Historical Association's publication, the *American Historical Review* (AHR) selects major articles from other journals in the field and cites them in its column of "Recent Publications." Thus, our first step in developing the list of journals for history was to count the number of articles selected from each history journal in a full year (1969)

[2] Once the journals to be analyzed in a given field had been selected, the adjustment criteria for foreign journals were not applied to those periodicals remaining in that field. Thus, the denominators reflecing the total citations and total source articles have not been completely adjusted for the presence of foreign journals. As a result the cumulative percentage of citations reported in these tables represents a *conservative* estimate of the coverage of quality work by American authors.

TABLE B-4   Journals Selected in History

Title	Selected (1969)[a]	Source Articles (1969)
1. *Agricultural History*	35	40
2. *Journal of Economic History*	35	31
3. *Current History*	30	88
4. *Church History*	30	31
5. *American Heritage*	28	58
6. *Journal of the History of Ideas*	27	37
7. *Historian*	27	26
8. *William and Mary Quarterly*	26	25
9. *Business History Review*	26	24
10. *American Historical Review*	24	24
11. *Hispanic American Historical Review*	23	20
12. *Journal of American History*	21	27
13. *American Quarterly*	20	37
14. *Pacific Historical Review*	20	22
15. *American Archivist*	17	24
16. *Labor History*	17	26
17. *Journal of Church and State*	17	22
18. *Isis*	16	36
19. *American Neptune*	16	21
20. *Journal of Modern History*	15	19
21. *Journal of Southern History*	11	17
22. *French Historical Studies*	8	24
23. *History and Theory*	8	25

[a] Articles published in 1969 that were cited in the *American Historical Review*'s "Recent Publications" section 1969-2/1971.

of AHR. This count yielded 212 journals from which one or more articles had been cited by AHR.

Time constraints and the nature of the study precluded using every journal in the AHR bibliography, so the following types were eliminated: foreign-language publications, organizational history journals (e.g., *Quaker History*), state history journals (e.g., *Georgia Historical Quarterly*), local history journals (e.g., *Rochester History*), history journals related to certain countries (e.g., *Liberian Studies Journal*), journals whose articles may be of interest to historians but that deal primarily with other topics (e.g., *Southern Speech Journal*), and certain types of specialized history journals.

The total list of journals (except for the excluded journals just mentioned, and without either the associated counts or an indication of how exactly they had been selected) were sent to three historians, who were asked to rate each journal in terms of whether it had major impact, minor impact, or no impact on the field of history. The results of this analysis substantiated the rank-ordering reflected in the AHR measure. Consequently, with one or two minor adjustments based on the reactions of these historians, the leading 23 journals in history as reflected in the AHR measure were selected for analysis.

Table B-4 presents the list of history journals selected, along with the measures developed in the study for rating and evaluating those journals.

Appendix C

Extra Analyses

A series of special analyses were conducted as a way of gaining additional perspectives on the Science Development program. They are described below.

ZERO-YEAR ANALYSIS

The argument can be made that plotting data on a year-by-year basis obscures effects because all grants were not awarded during the same year. That is, 1968 is the third year of some grants, the second year of others, and the first year of still others. To test this idea we conducted a special analysis in which the publication data for each of two fields, physics and chemistry, were realigned such that the year the grant was awarded consistently was defined as the "zero year." For each school data from the year after the grant was awarded were plotted at year "+1" regardless of which actual calendar year it had been; prefunding data from the year before the award were plotted as year"—1," etc. Then the data were aggregated for the USD and the medium control groups. We hoped to find previously obscured trends that reflected a consistent time lag between funding and subsequent publication. The experiment failed. We found the opposite: Effects that previously had been revealed were blurred and obscured in this analysis. The main reason was that the overall base rate in the field, as reported in Table 6-1, is a powerful factor in these curves. Thus, in doing the zero-year analysis we were placing the peak year of 1970 at different points, sometimes at year "+2, sometimes at year "+3," etc.

FEDERAL SUPPORT TO DEPARTMENTS

Some data on federal support to individual departments were available from the National Science Foundation for the fields of mathematics, physics, and chemistry. In addition to use of the 1968 information as an indicator of overall department funding in the residual analyses, a limited study was made of trends in this measure. The study had to be limited because the information was available for only four years: 1968, 1970, 1971, and 1972. The data were plotted in the hope that this might shed some light on the degree to which the momentum begun under Science Development funding might have resulted in increased federal support for the recipient departments. In all three fields, the USDs were receiving more funds than the medium controls in 1968. (This is not surprising since this measure included Science Development funds.) In chemistry the gap remained roughly the same in both the public and private sectors through 1972; in mathematics and physics the gap widened, an indication that the recipient departments in those fields were successful in attracting even more federal funds. Further inspection revealed that this trend was concentrated strictly in the public sector. In the private sector the gap narrowed by 1972.

CHANGES IN THE ACE FACULTY QUALITY RATINGS

A special comparison was made of the Cartter and Roose–Andersen scores of recipient institutions since the former was measured in a prefunding year and some have proposed the second as a crude measure of postfunding status. Of course, the USD and medium control groups began with virtually equal Cartter scores, since this was the basis on which the control group was selected. The analysis revealed no significant change. The Roose–Andersen scores of the two groups also were very close in all three fields. It appears from the other analyses in this volume that positive changes resulting from the grant occurred after a time lag such that the impact on the department's reputation simply could not be felt by the time the Roose–Andersen survey was taken.

IMPACT OF FUNDS FOR PERSONNEL, EQUIPMENT, AND FACILITIES

The amounts received by each recipient department for personnel, equipment, and facilities were added to the master file. As the reader will recall, in each of the multivariate analyses described in the text several partial correlations were computed, e.g., a partial between the criterion and a dummy variable indicating whether or not the school received a grant. At the same time three other partial correlations were generated to indicate the relative impact of the funds for personnel, equipment, and facilities. An analysis was conducted of this set of partials. The goal was to trace differential effects of funds for these three purposes—patterns that could serve as a guide for future federal funding policy. Without boring the reader with the gory details, suffice to say that this analysis was a disappointment. The pattern of these partial correlations did not yield new insights, although it was consistent with common sense expectations.

SCHOOL-BY-SCHOOL ANALYSIS: THE THRESHOLD THEORY

Once the entire master file of institutional data had been assembled, individual graphs were constructed to map changes in key variables for each field at each funded university, e.g., the chemistry department at the University of Maryland. Each graph plotted the data we had assembled on that institution over the 15-year period: faculty size, publication rate generated by the multivariate analysis, and so forth. The graphs for all USD recipients then were rank-ordered, to separate the "winners" from the "losers," on the basis of the departmental residual scores. The goal was to see if common factors could be detected that differentiated these two groups. Identification of such common factors might help future funding programs anticipate which schools would profit most from institutional support.

The *only* factor uncovered was the size of the Science Development grant, which, in turn, led to the hypothesis of a threshold effect; that is, it appeared that departments receiving above a given amount in the initial Science Development grant were much more likely to perform well, while those below that amount tended to do poorly. The amount varied from field to field (an initial award of $700,000 for mathematics and $800,000 for physics and chemistry.) As a follow-up on this notion, the USD recipients in each field were dichotomized at the threshold, and the trends on the criteria were analyzed separately for the two new groups. In Figures C-1, C-2, and C-3, publication data for those two groups, as well as for the medium control groups are plotted. Note that the "above threshold" USD recipients perform brilliantly. For example, in mathematics these schools seem to be moving into a catagory of excellence; they catch the high controls, a finding that is rarely matched elsewhere in this volume. In chemistry, the USD schools show a definite effect on publication rates, where before there was virtually none. Of the two experimental fields, chemistry had a larger portion of recipients with below threshold funding, suggesting one possible explanation for the poorer performance in this field reported earlier.

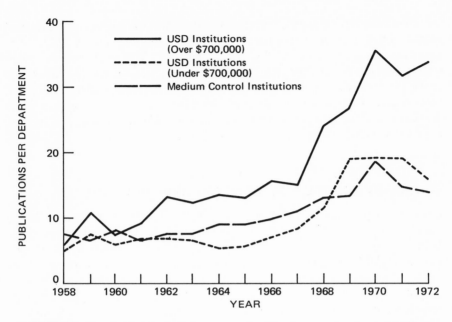

FIGURE C-1 Threshold analysis of departmental publication rates in science development and control institutions: mathematics.

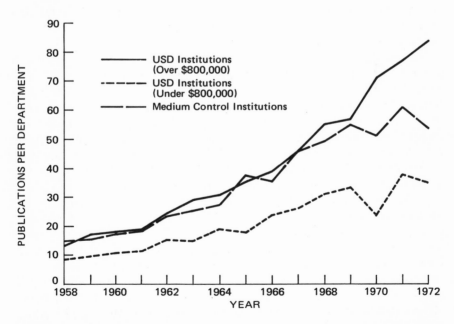

FIGURE C-2 Threshold analysis of departmental publication rates in science development and control institutions: physics.

181

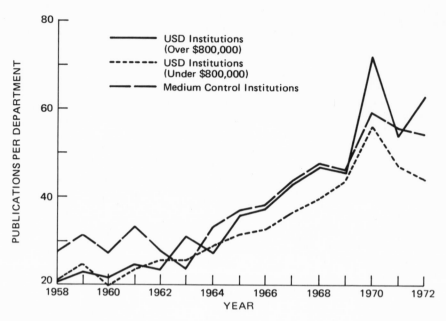

FIGURE C-3 Threshold analysis of departmental publication rates in science development and control institutions: chemistry.

PUBLICATION PER PERSON VS. FACULTY SIZE

Finally, we conducted an additional analysis in which publications per faculty member was plotted vs. faculty size for the four time points on which the size data were available. Examination of the slopes from these curves, while done with caution, shed some light on the mechanisms involved in the changes in productivity. The reader easily can replicate these graphs from the data presented in Chapters 5 and 6.

Extremely steep slopes indicate that per person productivity rose sharply while departmental size remained about the same; on the other hand, a relatively flat line indicates that per person productivity increased only slightly as the department grew. Inspection of these curves is a way of determining whether increased per person productivity is simply a monotonic function of larger departmental sizes or the result of having obtained a "critical mass."

Our conclusion based on these graphs and the review of the residual data discussed above is simply that the situation differed radically from school to school. A variety of patterns were found, including some funded (and control) departments in which per person productivity rose sharply while size increased slightly, indicating excellent departmental leadership.

182

NATIONAL BOARD ON GRADUATE EDUCATION PUBLICATIONS

Board Reports

1. *Graduate Education: Purposes, Problems and Potential,* November 1972, 18 pp.
2. *Doctorate Manpower Forecasts and Policy,* November 1973, 22 pp.
3. *Federal Policy Alternatives Toward Graduate Education,* March 1974, 127 pp.
4. *Science Development, University Development and the Federal Government,* June 1975, 48 pp.

Technical Reports

TR 1. *An Economic Perspective on the Evolution of Graduate Education,* by Stephen P. Dresch, March 1974, 76 pp.
TR 2. *Forecasting the Ph.D. Labor Market: Pitfalls for Policy,* by Richard Freeman and David W. Breneman, April 1974, 50 pp.
TR 3. *Graduate School Adjustments to the "New Depression" in Higher Education,* by David W. Breneman, with a *Commentary by the National Board on Graduate Education,* February 1975, 96 pp.
TR 4. *Science Development: An Evaluation Study,* by David E. Drew, June 1975, 182 pp.

Other Publications

An Annotated Bibliography on Graduate Education, 1971-1972, October 1972, 151 pp.

"Comment" on the Newman Task Force Report on the Federal Role in Graduate Education, June 1973, 13 pp.